C O O K I N G

F O R

F R I E N D S

A Guide to Planning

Potluck Meals

■

SUSAN MAHNKE PEERY

and GORDON PEERY

A   F I R E S I D E   B O O K
PUBLISHED BY SIMON & SCHUSTER
NEW YORK LONDON TORONTO SYDNEY TOKYO SINGAPORE

Fireside
Simon & Schuster Building
Rockefeller Center
1230 Avenue of the Americas
New York, New York 10020

FIRESIDE and colophon are registered trademarks
of Simon & Schuster

Designed by Bonni Leon
Manufactured in the United States of America

1   3   5   7   9   10   8   6   4   2

Library of Congress Cataloging in Publication Data
Peery, Susan Mahnke.
Cooking for friends: a guide to planning potluck meals/Susan
Mahnke Peery and Gordon Peery.
p.   cm.
1. Cookery.   2. Entertaining.   I. Peery, Gordon.   II. Title.
III. Title: Potluck meals.
TX714.P44   1991
641.5—dc20   91-4662
                                                                   CIP

ISBN 0-671-70967-4

For our children,
Molly and Spencer,
who might actually
like some of this
food some day.

And for Steve Zakon,
whose food and
friendship touch
so many circles.

C O N T E N T S

∎

One

APPETIZERS, MUNCHIES, AND DIPS   23

Contents

8

Four

RICE AND BEAN DISHES 87

Five

PASTA 99

Contents

Six

VEGETABLE DISHES 115

Seven

MEAT, POULTRY, AND SEAFOOD 127

Eight

SAVORY PIES 151

Nine

YEAST BREADS, QUICK BREADS, MUFFINS, AND MORE 165

Ten

DESSERTS 185

FOREWORD

■

When Susan and I were planning our wedding, we quickly came to the conclusion that we wanted to have a potluck supper for our wedding feast. We knew we wanted food to be an important part of the day's activities. And we knew that even if we had been able to hire the region's most exotic caterer, the food wouldn't be as good and as varied as what we could expect from our circle of friends.

Between us, we had had plenty of experience over the years in both attending and organizing potluck dinners. In the little town of Nelson, New Hampshire, where we live, we had been to many church and community gatherings. Traveling around the country playing New England contra dance music (one of my occupations), I had enjoyed excellent victuals at various pot-lucks held before dances. We had faith in the idea of a potluck, and we were not disappointed. What's more, to this day, people who were at our wedding remark on what a memorable meal it was.

It occurred to us at the time that if we had all the recipes for the food that was there that day, there would be a wonderful cookbook already made. The idea for this book was thereby conceived, and we thought of writing to everyone immediately for their recipes. Then other things sort of took over in the way that they do after you get married, and by the time we got serious enough to make a formal proposal for the book, we couldn't expect people to remember what they had brought. Still, it seemed that the book itself needed to be a sort of potluck event. We wrote to dozens of friends and relatives, asking for ideas and contributions. As the "hosts" it has been our job to fill in where things were needed, and to give balance and flow to the whole project. One of the best companions of food is friend-ship. The spirit of this book, therefore, comes from the many people who have shared their recipes with us. They are properly acknowl-edged throughout the book with their contributions.

We hope that this book brings new ideas and inspiration to circles of friends everywhere.

—G.P.

INTRODUCTION

■

POTLUCK SUPPERS—
THE BEAUTY OF IT ALL

Potluck gatherings are among the most congenial of all social events, combining informality, good food, no huge amount of work for any one person, and the element of serendipity that comes from not knowing exactly what the luck of the pot will be!

Of course, as a host you can manage the variety of food that will appear on your table by assigning categories or even specific dishes to certain people. "Please come to a potluck supper at our house next Saturday and bring a salad" (or a pasta dish, or some brownies) is certainly an acceptable invitation to issue. You may decide to provide the main course and ask guests to fill in with side dishes and desserts. Community organizations sponsoring potluck suppers often have sign-up sheets to insure the proper quantities and types of food.

But if you don't mind inviting a certain amount of risk into your life, be nonspecific in your invitations and let your guests be creative. If you end up with a bountiful spread that only includes two of the four basic food groups, no one will be permanently malnourished.

HOW TO HOST A POTLUCK

If you are inviting people to your home, it's usually easiest for everyone if you as the host provide the utensils (including extra serving spoons), napkins, plates, cups, ice, and beverages. Your supply of salt and pepper, ketchup, mustard, and other condiments may also be drawn on. Make sure you have enough coffee and cream; also, consider the needs of any children who might be coming and have juice and milk on hand. If you are in the habit of serving substantial amounts of wine or other alcohol, you might want to share the burden with a guest who doesn't like to cook (or whose cooking you don't like).

It's helpful if you give your guests a target time for serving the meal so that people can anticipate what condition their casserole or salad will be in by then. Ask guests if they will need to use your stove so you can choreograph the reheatings. Make room in your refrigerator, or have a couple of picnic coolers and extra ice on hand.

Unless you will have a small number of guests (fewer than eight, for instance), it usually works best to serve the meal as a buffet arranged in some logical linear style.

HOW TO BE A GUEST AT A POTLUCK

The most important thing is to bring something tasty. It's usually not necessary to make a huge quantity, since potluckers tend to take a little bit of everything. What might serve six if it's the only thing in sight will easily stretch to feed twelve or fifteen at a potluck.

The next most important thing is to bring something appropriate —i.e., a dish that can be served in multiple portions and eaten with a spoon or a fork off a paper plate balanced on one's lap. Appropriate also means food that has a half-life of longer than a few minutes. For this reason, soufflé and baked alaska are not the best choices for a potluck. Anything that takes a lot of last-minute preparation— stir-fries, broiled toppings, steaks medium-rare—will task the capacity of your host's kitchen, not to mention his or her patience.

Bring any necessary garnishes or accompaniments. If you bring dinner rolls, also bring butter and a butter knife or two. Salads will need dressings and maybe even croutons. If possible, dress salads at the last minute so they won't get soggy. (I can't help but think, as I write this last sentence, that I adopted this same rule for myself when my children were babies—I never dressed to go out until the last possible moment!)

Assume responsibility for keeping your dish at the proper temperature. Use insulated carriers to keep food warm or cold. Our friend Kathy Miller visited her neighbor, Edith Chase, in East Alstead, New Hampshire, to trace her pattern for a quilted casserole carrier (see drawing below). It is easy to make, useful, and pretty; you can adapt it to fit your favorite crockery and cookware.

Keep track of any bowls, trays, and utensils you bring and don't forget to tote them back home again.

Finally, enough people need to be on a clean-up crew so that no one gets stuck restoring order alone.

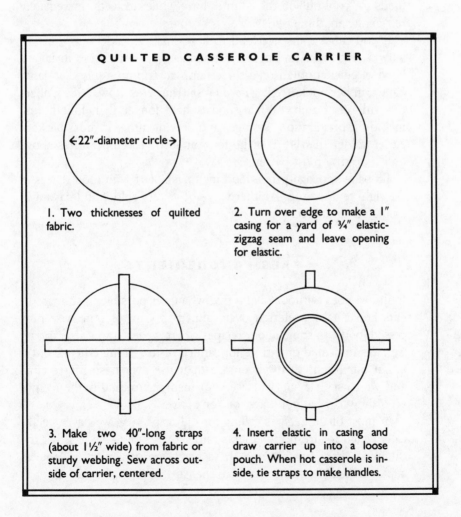

QUILTED CASSEROLE CARRIER

←22″-diameter circle→

1. Two thicknesses of quilted fabric.

2. Turn over edge to make a 1″ casing for a yard of ¾″ elastic-zigzag seam and leave opening for elastic.

3. Make two 40″-long straps (about 1½″ wide) from fabric or sturdy webbing. Sew across outside of carrier, centered.

4. Insert elastic in casing and draw carrier up into a loose pouch. When hot casserole is inside, tie straps to make handles.

THE QUESTION OF SPOILAGE

Protein foods—meats, seafood, eggs—are the main culprits in episodes of food poisoning. This is because the pathogenic bacteria—primarily, salmonella and staphylococcus—that multiply enough to make us sick require moisture, warmth, and a host that is neither too acidic nor too alkaline to support bacteria growth. For example, flour is too dry, fruits too acidic, vegetables too akaline. These disease-causing bacteria grow fast and furious after about four hours in agreeable surroundings.

Most of the rules for avoiding food poisoning apply to the preparation of food. Scrupulous cleanliness, especially in dealing with raw meats, and rapid cooling of all cooked foods are essential. Basically, hot foods should be kept hot, cold foods cold. Do not allow foods to "cool off" on the counter for a while. Instead, immediately refrigerate anything perishable.

If you must transport food to a potluck, consider the time involved and make an appropriate choice. Do not decide to take a bowl of chicken salad on a three-hour car trip on a July day. Janet Bailey, in her book *Keeping Food Fresh* (Harper & Row, 1989), offers this rule of thumb: "When food is held longer than four hours, including preparation, storage, and serving time, it must be kept either colder than 45°F or hotter than 140°F. Temperatures above 165°F destroy most bacteria."

To pack spoilage-prone food for travel, start with food that is at the right temperature—either very hot or very cold—and pack it in insulated containers.

FRESH INGREDIENTS

It almost goes without saying that whenever possible fresh ingredients are usually preferred over canned, frozen, or otherwise processed foods. In some of our recipes where we felt it was appropriate we have indicated quantities for canned or frozen ingredients, but it is not our intention to encourage their use over fresh ingredients, and we trust that you will use your instincts to modify the recipes according to what you have, or don't have.

In most of the recipes calling for dill or parsley, we have specifically called for fresh ingredients rather than dried. We feel that the difference is significant and these herbs are generally available at supermarkets if not directly from the garden. Other herbs are not as available in fresh form and for this reason we do not specify fresh, though we certainly recommend that fresh herbs be used any time they are available. As a general rule (and one that you should interpret liberally), it is better to use less of dried herbs than you would of fresh.

COVERED AND UNCOVERED

In dishes that require oven time, we have generally made a recommendation as to whether or not they should be covered during baking. In most cases, where we have recommended that a casserole be cooked uncovered, it is so the top can be browned and crisped. However, if you are going to reheat the dish later, you may want to do the first baking with the cover on to avoid drying out the food.

—S.P.

One

APPETIZERS,

MUNCHIES,

AND DIPS

■

In terms of function, appetizer items at a potluck are no different from the other food items there. Technically, appetizers are more likely to be finger foods, which means that they can be eaten as one is going through the potluck line, saving valuable space on the plate for other things such as casserole items.

In many cases, the recipes in this section will require less time and effort than those elsewhere, so the hurried or harried potlucker might browse through here first. Ultimately, we hope that this chapter will contribute to expanding the scope of potluck suppers; our experience has been that breads, casseroles, salads, and desserts predominate.

FRUIT PLATTER

•

from Julie Brody

NEWTON, MASSACHUSETTS

2 or 3 melons of different colors
1 or 2 kinds of berry-sized fruits
of different colors, e.g., red and
green grapes—or my favorite,
strawberries with a handful of
bright-orange kumquats

Fresh mint or edible flowers for
garnish
1 exceptionally nice plate, at least
13 inches across (this is the key
ingredient!)

Slice the melons, then cut each slice into halves or thirds. Leave the skin on, so guests can use it as a "handle" to eat the melon without utensils. Wash the berries or other fruits and the garnishes, and pat them dry. Cut the grape stems into convenient-sized bunches. Arrange everything on the plate in a pleasing design. Don't worry—it's hard to go wrong.

When shopping for ingredients, think about who the other guests will be. If I know toddlers will be at the party, I might add a couple of bananas and omit the grapes because they can cause choking.

This is my favorite thing to take to potluck suppers. It looks beautiful and it always gets eaten. It's a guilt-free antidote for that leaden feeling that overtakes weak-willed potluckers who can't resist trying a little bit of everything.

—J.B.

CHEESE WAFERS

—————
■

2 cups grated sharp Cheddar
  cheese
¼ cup unsalted butter, at room
  temperature
½ cup flour

1½ teaspoons Worcestershire
  sauce
1 teaspoon salt
¼ teaspoon cayenne pepper

In a bowl, combine the cheese and butter until well blended. Stir in the flour, Worcestershire, salt, and cayenne. Shape into a long roll 1 inch in diameter. Refrigerate for at least 3 hours, until firm.

Cut the roll into thin slices and place on ungreased baking sheets. Bake in a preheated oven at 450°F for 5 minutes, until lightly browned. Makes 4 dozen.

CHEESE STRAWS

—————
■

1 cup flour
1½ teaspoons baking powder
½ teaspoon salt
2 tablespoons butter

½ cup shredded sharp Cheddar
  cheese
⅓ cup cold water

Sift the flour, baking powder, and salt into a medium bowl. Cut in the butter with a pastry blender until the mixture is crumbly. Add the cheese and toss until well blended. Sprinkle the water over the mixture. Mix lightly with a fork until the pastry just holds together.

Roll out on a floured surface into a 12-by-10-inch rectangle. Cut in half lengthwise, then cut each half crosswise into ½-inch strips. Twist the individual strips into spirals and place on ungreased cookie sheets.

Bake in a preheated oven at 425°F for 10 minutes or until light golden. Cool on wire racks.

CUMIN-GET-IT CRACKERS

■

1 cup whole wheat flour
2 tablespoons unbleached flour
2 tablespoons millet seed
½ teaspoon baking powder
½ teaspoon baking soda
½ teaspoon ground cumin

¼ teaspoon salt
2 tablespoons wheat germ
Coarse salt to taste (optional)
2 tablespoons unsalted butter
4 tablespoons plain yogurt or
  buttermilk

Mix together all the dry ingredients except the coarse salt. Cut in the butter. Add just enough yogurt or buttermilk to make the dough stick together. Knead the dough gently for 30 seconds and roll out on a floured surface to ¹⁄₁₆ inch thick. The crackers may be cut individually with a floured cookie cutter or biscuit cutter, or scored with a pastry wheel. Gather any leftover dough, roll out, and cut again.

Transfer the crackers to a buttered baking sheet and prick them with a fork. Sprinkle with coarse salt if desired. Bake in a preheated oven at 450°F for 8 to 10 minutes or until golden.

The quantity of crackers depends on the size you make them. This recipe will make about 60 round crackers, 2 inches in diameter.

WALKING TOSTADA

■

from Judy and Mike Patenaude

MADISON, WISCONSIN

"This recipe takes a bit of preparation (maybe the day or evening before) but can be assembled quickly just before the potluck. It is served cold, so no extra reheating paraphernalia is needed. The tostada is big and aesthetically most appealing. It is liked by young and old and has proved to be a great international and intergenerational success.

"Mike and I first started making this when we had our first [American Field Service] exchange student in 1984. The AFS hosting group put on many gatherings for the district exchange kids that usually culminated in a big potluck with the kids and their host families. Since there were a couple of weekends a month we seemed to have some "thing" to go to—bring Isabelle to or pick her up from —we became known to our friends as the 'Potluck Patenaudes'!"

—Judy Patenaude

One 31-ounce can refried beans
2 avocados, chopped
2 to 3 tomatoes, chopped
Two 6-ounce cans pitted black
  olives
5 scallions, chopped

One 8-ounce jar mild taco sauce
4 to 8 ounces hot picante sauce
1 cup coarsely grated Colby
  cheese
1 cup coarsely grated Monterey
  Jack cheese

Spread the beans evenly on a large round platter. Layer with the remaining items in the order given. Serve with tostadas or nacho chips.

TIROPITAS (ΤΥΡΟΠΗΤΑ) AND WORKING WITH PHYLLO PASTRY

Tiropitas are triangular turnovers made with phyllo pastry. (If you have not worked with phyllo pastry before, please read about it in chapter 8, Savory Pies.)

While some of the recipes we have here are for traditional types of tiropitas, we became intrigued with the possibilities and experimented extensively. We share the results of our more successful endeavors here.

Our method of creating a tiropita is to start with a single sheet of thawed phyllo that is brushed with melted butter, folded in half lengthwise, and then buttered on that surface. The ingredients are then placed near the bottom of the sheet, and a triangular fold is made over the ingredients. Some effort will probably be needed to keep the filling from slipping out the side for the first few folds. The folding continues, in the same way that a flag is folded up. Brush more butter on the new outside layer that emerges after each fold. When the top is reached, seal any loose edges with a brushing of butter.

The tiropitas should be set on greased cookie sheets, and each one should be pricked with a sharp pointed knife (a fork will not penetrate the soft phyllo without pushing it down) to let moisture escape.

This procedure can be used for all of the following tiropita recipes, plus any that you want to experiment with. In all cases the proportions are for a full (twenty-six sheets) eight-ounce box of frozen phyllo dough, nine by thirteen inches. They are based on using approximately two tablespoons of filling per sheet. If you want to make a variety, you can cut the proportions into one half or one third, and make two or three different fillings. When you reach the halfway point of using the phyllo, check your filling. If there's more than half of it left, go a little heavier, and if there's less than half, use less filling per sheet to stretch it out.

The most important thing of all: Be sure to have everything ready to go before you open the package of phyllo.

Most of these tiropitas can be served hot, at room temperature, or cold. They will reheat best in a conventional oven (as opposed to a microwave oven). They can also be constructed in advance, frozen, and baked later (add ten minutes to the baking time).

HOW TO FOLD A TIROPITA

1.

2.

3.

4.

5.

THE TIROPITA RECIPES

All the recipes are for one 8-ounce package of frozen phyllo pastry. (Please read about phyllo on page 151 in the Savory Pies chapter and about Tiropitas on page 28.) The pastry needs to be thawed in advance. A quarter pound of melted butter is needed for all the recipes for brushing the pastry sheets and greasing the pans. All the recipes require baking in a preheated oven at 350°F for approximately thirty minutes or until the phyllo begins to turn golden brown.

BROCCOLI TIROPITA

•

Two 10-ounce packages frozen
 chopped broccoli, thawed and
 squeezed dry
1 pound feta cheese, crumbled
1 small onion, diced

2 eggs
2 teaspoons dried oregano
One 8-ounce package phyllo
 pastry, thawed (see page 151)

Cook the broccoli only if necessary to accommodate thawing, then drain well. Mix all the filling ingredients together. Use 2 tablespoons of filling for each tiropita. Spoon onto the prepared phyllo, assemble, and bake according to the directions on pages 28–29.

PEPPERONI TIROPITA

•

The quantities listed are what you should have on hand. You'll probably end up with a few extra olives and maybe a little extra pepperoni.

One 8-ounce stick pepperoni, thinly sliced
One 7-ounce jar pimiento-stuffed green olives, sliced

1¾ cups grated Cheddar cheese
One 8-ounce package phyllo pastry, thawed (see page 151)

For each tiropita set down 2 slices of pepperoni first, then 2 sliced olives, and top with 1 tablespoon of cheese. Press the cheese a little bit to hold everything in place before folding the prepared phyllo. Assemble and bake according to the directions on pages 28–29. This recipe is not recommended for freezing.

CHEESY TIROPITA

•

¾ pound Muenster cheese, coarsely grated
8 ounces feta cheese, crumbled
1 pint small-curd cottage cheese
2 eggs, slightly beaten

3 tablespoons chopped parsley
¼ teaspoon pepper
One 8-ounce package phyllo pastry, thawed (see page 151)

Mix the cheeses together until well combined. Stir in the eggs, parsley, and pepper. Spoon onto the prepared phyllo, assemble, and bake according to the directions on pages 28–29.

MEDITIROPITA

·

2 cups sliced mushrooms
¼ cup diced green pepper
¼ cup diced red or yellow pepper
¼ cup diced onion
2 cloves garlic, pressed
1 tablespoon olive oil
Salt to taste

1 cup pitted and chopped Greek
 olives
One 8-ounce package phyllo
 pastry, thawed (see page 151)
1 cup grated mozzarella cheese
½ cup grated Parmesan cheese

Sauté the mushrooms, pepper, onion, and garlic in the oil until tender. Drain off any excess liquid. Season with salt.

Add the olives to the vegetable mixture. Spoon onto the prepared phyllo and top with the cheese—a shy 2 teaspoons of mozzarella and a shy 1 teaspoon of Parmesan per tiropita. Assemble and bake according to the directions on pages 28–29.

APPLE TIROPITA

·

6 medium apples, peeled and
 chopped (about 2½ cups)
4 teaspoons lemon juice
1 cup chopped dates

½ cup golden raisins
½ cup brown sugar
One 8-ounce package phyllo
 pastry, thawed (see page 151)

Toss the apples with the lemon juice, then add the dates, raisins, and sugar and toss to combine. Spoon about 1½ tablespoons of the filling onto the prepared phyllo. Assemble and bake according to the directions on pages 28–29.

LAMB AND CHUTNEY TIROPITA

—— •

1 pound ground lamb
1 small onion, chopped
2 cloves garlic, chopped
½ teaspoon ground cumin
½ cup pine nuts
½ cup chutney (for Rhubarb
  Chutney, see page 44, or use
  Major Grey or other standard
  brand)

Salt and pepper to taste
One 8-ounce package phyllo
  pastry, thawed (see page 151)

Sauté the lamb with the onion and garlic, stirring to break up the meat, until the lamb is no longer pink. Remove from the pan with a slotted spoon to drain off as much grease as possible. Combine the lamb, onion, and garlic with the cumin, pine nuts, and chutney in a medium bowl. Season with salt and pepper. Let cool slightly, then fill the prepared phyllo with 1 heaping tablespoon per tiropita. Assemble and bake according to the directions on pages 28–29.

YANKEE TIROPITA

·

2½ cups small, thin apple slices
½ teaspoon ground cinnamon
¼ teaspoon ground cloves
⅛ teaspoon ground nutmeg
⅛ teaspoon ground allspice

1 tablespoon sugar
1¾ cups grated Cheddar cheese
One 8-ounce package phyllo
   pastry, thawed (see page 151)

In a bowl, mix all the filling ingredients together except the cheese. On each prepared phyllo sheet, place a heaping tablespoon of the apple filling, and top with a level tablespoon of cheese. Assemble and bake according to the directions on pages 28–29.

This tastes best when it is cold.

Damn the tiropitas and full speed ahead!

MARINATED CARROTS

·

from Jean deLongchamp

FITZWILLIAM, NEW HAMPSHIRE

2 pounds carrots, peeled and
   sliced lengthwise
1 large onion, sliced
1 green pepper, diced
One 10¾-ounce can tomato soup
   (undiluted)

½ cup vegetable oil
½ cup sugar
⅔ cup vinegar
1 teaspoon prepared mustard
1 teaspoon Worcestershire sauce

Cook the carrots in boiling water (or steam) until crisp-tender. Cool. In a saucepan, heat the soup, oil, sugar, vinegar, mustard, and Worcestershire, lightly stirring to combine. Pour over the vegetables. (The onion and pepper remain uncooked.) Chill overnight and serve.

CARROT PÂTÉ

.

Genessee Bondurant of Martinsburg, West Virginia, was the snack caterer at Augusta Dance Week in 1990. The dance week is held at Davis and Elkins College in Elkins, West Virginia, and the daily meal fare is cafeteria food. Even if that had been good, Genessee's evening snacks would have stood out for their quality. As it was, her snacks were not only delicious, they were a lifesaver, and this particular recipe was the hit of the week.

1½ pounds carrots
½ small onion, finely minced
2 cloves garlic, finely minced
2 tablespoons tahini
2 tablespoons white miso
1 tablespoon extra-virgin olive oil

1 tablespoon minced fresh basil
1 tablespoon minced fresh oregano
½ tablespoon minced fresh parsley
½ tablespoon minced fresh chives

Peel and cut up the carrots any way you choose and cook them until soft. Mash them up with a fork or other manual masher— a food processor runs the risk of overdoing it. Mix with all the other ingredients and refrigerate for at least 2 hours before serving.

For a milder flavor, sauté the garlic and onion.

TOMATOES AND BASIL

·

from Rich Hart and Wendy Rannenberg

AMHERST, NEW HAMPSHIRE

Some food is so simple, it might seem out of place in a cookbook. Nevertheless, if you have the fresh ingredients, you will be well praised for bringing the following dish to a potluck.

Rich and Wendy point out that in New Hampshire only the months of August and September lend themselves to making this possible. Areas with longer growing seasons can supply the ingredients for a longer time, but it should really be limited to that: Don't make this with store-bought produce—it just won't be the same.

*3 large Beefsteak tomatoes,
 ripened to perfection
½ cup loosely packed basil leaves,
 freshly harvested and washed*

2 tablespoons best-quality olive oil

Slice the tomatoes about ¼ inch thick and arrange artistically on a white plate. Chop up the basil and sprinkle it over the tomatoes. Sprinkle the olive oil over, varying the quantity to your taste. Let set for 30 minutes before serving.

If the size of the plate requires more than 1 layer of tomatoes, sprinkle the basil and oil over each layer before starting the next.

CRAB-STUFFED CHERRY TOMATOES

•

15 ripe cherry tomatoes, washed
¼ pound crabmeat
2 teaspoons plain yogurt
1 teaspoon chopped fresh parsley
1 teaspoon finely diced onion

½ teaspoon Worcestershire sauce
Dash each of salt, pepper,
  paprika, thyme, celery seed, and
  dill

Core the tops of the tomatoes and set aside. Combine the remaining ingredients and mix gently. Spoon the mixture into the tomatoes, extending over the tops by ½ inch. Sprinkle with additional paprika or additional parsley. This can be served cold as it is or baked in a preheated oven at 375°F for 10 minutes.

The filling can also be used for crackers or for stuffing other vegetables such as celery.

SPICY ALMONDS

•

3 tablespoons butter
2 teaspoons salt
1 pound blanched almonds

3 tablespoons Worcestershire
  sauce
Dash of Tabasco sauce

In a large saucepan, melt the butter, stir in the salt, and add the almonds. Stir so that they are thoroughly coated.

Add the remaining ingredients and stir again. When everything is well mixed, turn the mixture into a shallow baking pan. Bake in a preheated oven at 300°F for 30 minutes, stirring every so often.

SAUSAGE-AND-CHEESE BALLS

•

from Sheila Datzman

BURWOOD, TENNESSEE

1 pound bulk sausage
1½ cups Bisquick
8 ounces cream cheese, at room
    temperature

1 cup grated Cheddar cheese
Dash of Tabasco sauce

Mix everything together and make into walnut-sized patties. Bake on an ungreased baking sheet in a preheated oven at 275°F for 20 to 25 minutes. Makes 40 to 45.

CONFETTI CHEESE BALL

•

16 ounces cream cheese, at room
    temperature
2 cups grated Cheddar cheese
1 tablespoon chopped pimiento
1 tablespoon chopped green
    pepper

1 tablespoon Worcestershire sauce
1 teaspoon lemon juice
Dash of Tabasco sauce
Dash of salt
½ cup finely chopped nuts

Combine the cream cheese and Cheddar cheese until well blended. Add the remaining ingredients except the nuts and mix well. Chill. Shape into a ball about softball-sized, then roll in the nuts to cover.

This is very good with rye crackers.

BABA GANOUSH

•

1 large eggplant
6 cloves garlic, minced
1 teaspoon salt
½ cup tahini

3 tablespoons lemon juice
½ cup chopped parsley
⅛ teaspoon cayenne pepper

Prick the eggplant with a fork and roast in a preheated oven at 400°F for about 30 minutes or until tender. When the eggplant has cooled sufficiently, peel off the skin and chop the flesh into large pieces (about 1-inch cubes).

In a blender, combine all the other ingredients and begin blending. Add the eggplant pieces and blend until the mixture is smooth. Garnish with additional fresh parsley and serve with pita bread or vegetables.

TAPENADE

•

A rich olive spread for french bread or for dipping raw vegetables or hard-cooked eggs.

1 cup pitted black olives cured in
   oil
3 cloves garlic
One 2-ounce can anchovies in oil,
   drained

1 small can tuna in oil, drained
¼ cup capers, drained well
¼ cup plus 2 teaspoons olive oil
1 teaspoon Dijon mustard
Tabasco sauce to taste

In a blender or food processor, blend the olives and garlic together, then add the anchovies, tuna, capers, ¼ cup olive oil, mustard, and hot pepper sauce gradually until the mixture is smooth. Place the Tapenade in a bowl and pour the remaining 2 teaspoons of oil over to seal. Cover tightly with plastic wrap and refrigerate for at least half a day and up to 2 weeks.

YOGURT-CHEESE SPREAD

·

2 quarts plain yogurt
½ cup finely minced scallions
¼ cup chopped chives
1 tablespoon dried dill
1 tablespoon finely chopped
 pimiento

1½ cups coarsely chopped
 walnuts
⅛ teaspoon pepper

Line a colander with several layers of dampened cheesecloth. Set the colander in a larger pan and place the yogurt in the cheesecloth. Refrigerate overnight. The moisture will drain out of the yogurt and the volume will be reduced by half.

Place the yogurt in a bowl, reserving the liquid. If it seems too thick to work, add back some of the liquid that drained off. Stir in the remaining ingredients and shape into a mound.

This can be served with pita triangles or crackers or used to stuff celery, endive spears, or anything else that will bear stuffing.

CRAB-AVOCADO DIP

·

6 to 8 ounces crabmeat
1 large avocado
1 tablespoon lemon juice
1 tablespoon finely diced onion
1 teaspoon Worcestershire sauce

¼ teaspoon salt
8 ounces cream cheese, at room
 temperature
¼ cup sour cream

Shred the crabmeat. In a blender, combine the avocado, lemon juice, onion, Worcestershire sauce, and salt. Blend until smooth. Add the cream cheese and sour cream and blend well. Remove mixture to bowl, then fold in crabmeat. Cover and chill.

Serve with veggies and/or chips.

HANCOCK HOT DIP

.

from Deb Navas

PETERBOROUGH, NEW HAMPSHIRE

16 ounces cream cheese, at room
  temperature
½ pint sour cream
2½ ounces dried beef, chopped

¼ envelope onion soup mix
½ small green pepper, chopped
Dash of Worcestershire sauce
½ cup chopped walnuts

Mix everything together except the walnuts and pour into a small baking dish. Sprinkle walnuts on top. Bake uncovered in a preheated oven at 325°F for 30 minutes.

CUCUMBER-YOGURT DIP

.

2 cups plain yogurt
1 large clove garlic, pressed
½ teaspoon salt
2 cups quartered and thinly sliced
  cucumbers

1 teaspoon finely chopped fresh
  mint
1 teaspoon finely chopped fresh
  dill

Stir the yogurt, garlic, and salt together in a bowl. Add the cucumber slices and mint. Chill for at least an hour. Top with the dill before serving.

NOTE This is particularly good with Cumin-Get-It Crackers (page 26).

SUMMER GARDEN DIP

•

from Mary DesRosiers,

HARRISVILLE, NEW HAMPSHIRE

HERB BLEND
3 tablespoons fresh dill
2 teaspoons fresh basil
1 teaspoon fresh thyme

Equal parts plain yogurt and
mayonnaise

Mary writes: "First, send the kids out to the garden to pick some dill, basil, thyme, etc. That should give you enough time to wash and slice some carrots, broccoli, cauliflower, cukes, or what you have.

"Mix equal amounts of yogurt and mayonnaise. Then mix in about a quarter of a cup of diced herbs and maybe a dash of salt. Put it in a sealed container if you're traveling, otherwise a bowl will do.

"This dip is quite tasty and can be adapted with curry powder, cayenne, garlic, etc., to suit a variety of palates. It's also great with chips. When you get to the potluck, all the kids will be starving and the grown-ups will be socializing and slow about serving up the food. You can be the hero of the evening by producing your veggies and dip. The kids can help themselves and get a wholesome start on the meal while everyone else heats up the beans and apple crisp."

GUACAMOLE

There are two basic types of guacamole: the chunky kind and the creamy kind. While the chunky variety is more earthy and can be scooped up easily with a chip, the creamy variety is a little bit easier to hold on a carrot or celery stick.

How you go about preparing the guacamole will have something to do with the stage of ripeness of the avocado, which is the key ingredient. A soft avocado can be easily mashed with a fork and the other ingredients chopped up by hand. A less-ripe avocado may require blending even if you are making the chunky variety.

Finally, the ingredients are highly flexible, depending on your taste or the tastes of those you want to please. We recommend using at least a lot of garlic, and possibly more, but that's really up to you. Once you've mashed the avocado, improvise. Here's how we do it.

CHUNKY GUACAMOLE

•

2 large or 3 small ripe avocados
½ cup sour cream or plain yogurt
½ cup diced onion
½ cup chopped tomato
¼ cup diced green pepper
1 tablespoon chopped parsley
3 cloves garlic, pressed

2 teaspoons chili powder
Dash of cayenne pepper
1 tablespoon lemon juice
1 teaspoon lime juice
1 tablespoon olive oil
½ teaspoon salt

Skin the avocados and mash or blend until smooth. Add the other ingredients and mix by hand until everything is well combined. Refrigerate until ready to serve or travel.

TIP If you're making the guacamole well in advance, reserve some of the sour cream or yogurt and spread it over the top. This will keep the green from browning, and you can mix it in just before serving.

CREAMY GUACAMOLE

·

2 large or 3 small ripe avocados
½ cup diced onion
2 tablespoons tomato paste
3 cloves garlic, pressed
2 teaspoons chili powder
Dash of cayenne pepper
1 tablespoon lemon juice

1 teaspoon lime juice
1 tablespoon olive oil
½ teaspoon salt
½ cup sour cream or plain yogurt
½ cup mayonnaise
1 tablespoon chopped parsley

Skin the avocados and cut into chunks. Blend in a food processor with everything but the last 3 ingredients until well mixed. Add the sour cream or yogurt, mayonnaise, and parsley. Whirrr for about 15 seconds more in the food processor, or whisk in by hand. Refrigerate until ready to serve or travel.

CHUTNEY

Expensive to purchase but relatively simple and inexpensive to make, chutney is a "transforming" condiment. Add it to a ham sandwich, fold some into a chicken salad, serve it beside some gussied-up rice, and you'll create a whole new taste. The two recipes that follow use local, easy-to-find ingredients.

RHUBARB CHUTNEY

·

6 cups diced rhubarb
2 cups sugar
1½ cups raisins

¾ cup chopped onion
½ cup vinegar
1 teaspoon salt

2 teaspoons ground ginger
1 teaspoon ground cinnamon

1 teaspoon ground allspice
½ cup chopped walnuts

*P*ut all the ingredients except the walnuts in a heavy 4-quart kettle and bring slowly to a boil. Simmer, stirring frequently, until thickened (about 1 hour, depending on how humid the day is). Stir in the walnuts. Pour into sterilized jars and pour a layer of melted paraffin over the top to make a seal, or can using a boiling-water-bath method (see page 125). Store in a cool place.

The chutney may also be poured into a container and stored, covered, in the refrigerator for up to a month. Makes 4 to 5 cups.

PEACH CHUTNEY
•

1 pound peaches, peeled and
 chopped
½ pound dried apricots, chopped
1 pound Granny Smith apples,
 peeled and chopped
1 large onion, chopped
3 cloves garlic, minced
1 cup raisins
1½ cups cider vinegar
1 cup water

1½ cups brown sugar
1 teaspoon salt
1 teaspoon ground cinnamon
1 teaspoon ground cumin
½ teaspoon ground coriander
2 teaspoons ground ginger
½ teaspoon ground cloves
½ teaspoon ground allspice
¼ cup finely chopped crystallized
 ginger

*C*ombine all the ingredients in a heavy nonreactive pot, bring to a boil, and simmer until thick and syrupy, about 1 hour. Stir often. Use canning directions for Rhubarb Chutney above. Store in the refrigerator or a cool place. This tastes best after 3 or 4 weeks, when the flavors have blended. Makes 4 to 5 cups.

Two

S O U P S

·

Soups are less common at potluck meals than other one-dish recipes. This is mostly because soups require a separate cup or bowl for each serving, and they also tend to be temperature-sensitive. (Or maybe *we* are just being finicky, but we do prefer soup to be either piping hot or what our daughter calls "piping cold.")

However, there are ways around these problems. If you bring soup to a potluck, also bring a stack of heat-resistant cups, some plastic spoons, and a ladle. Make sure you will be able to heat up a soup that needs it or keep a cold soup cold, so they can be served at optimum temperature. With any luck, there will be lots of good crusty bread to accompany your soup.

GINGERED CREAM-OF-CARROT SOUP

•

1 medium onion
1 clove garlic
2 tablespoons butter
1½ pounds carrots
1 quart chicken broth (homemade
  or canned)

Salt and pepper to taste
One 2-inch chunk ginger, peeled
  and grated (about 2 tablespoons)
2 cups half-and-half
Chopped parsley for garnish

Peel and chop the onion and garlic. Melt the butter in a 4-quart pot and sauté the onion and garlic until tender. Peel and chop the carrots and add to the saucepan along with 2 cups of the chicken broth. Cover and cook until the carrots are tender. Puree the vegetables and broth in a blender or food processor and return to the pot. Stir in the remaining 2 cups of broth, salt and pepper, and the grated ginger. Simmer gently for about 10 minutes. Stir in the half-and-half and heat, but do not allow to boil. Taste and add salt or additional ginger if desired. Sprinkle the parsley on top of the soup just before serving.

TAVERN SOUP

•

I learned to make this soup in my early days as a restaurant cook. It was a big hit, and as time went on I became increasingly daring about what I would put into it. The only restriction I would recommend is to avoid peppers and go light on tomatoes. Below are what I consider to be ideal proportions, but most other vegetables will also work well, so use up what you have

—G.P.

1 pound carrots	2 quarts chicken broth
1 stalk celery	1 pound Cheddar cheese, grated
1 zucchini	One 12-ounce bottle good-quality
½ head cauliflower	beer
1 large onion	Chopped scallions for garnish

Cut the vegetables into 1-inch chunks. Put the chicken broth in a large kettle and add the vegetables. Bring to a broil and then reduce to a gentle boil for 15 minutes or so, until the vegetables are tender. Let this cool for as long as you can—it can even be refrigerated and taken out to finish later.

Ladle the vegetables and broth into a blender and puree. Empty the blender into a large kettle. This will take several blending sessions. If you run out of broth and the vegetables are too thick to puree, just add some of what you've already blended back into it.

When this is done, heat the vegetable-broth blend. When it gets to just under boiling, stir in the cheese and cook for 10 minutes, stirring regularly. Slowly pour in the beer and stir. Raise the heat to high and cook for 15 minutes, stirring occasionally. Sprinkle in chopped scallions before serving.

BASEBALL BAT SOUP

·

Carolyn Edwards sent us this recipe—she said she got it from her dear friend Sally Thursby, and it dates back to the days when Carolyn and Sally were partners in a sidewalk lunch business called Out to Lunch, in Hanover, New Hampshire.

1 baseball-bat-sized zucchini with skin, cut up (or 3–4 medium size)	*1 teaspoon salt*
	½ teaspoon dried chervil
	5 cloves garlic
½ cup water	*1 to 3 cups chicken broth*
Butter the size of an egg (about ¼ cup)	*Sour cream or plain yogurt for garnish*

*I*n a heavy 4-quart pot, combine the zucchini, water, butter, salt, chervil, and garlic. Cook, covered, until the zucchini is very soft. Puree in a blender or food processor to make a mushy pulp. To every 3 cups of pulp add 1 cup of chicken broth. Serve hot or cold with a plop of sour cream or yogurt. Serves a variable number depending on the size of the zucchini.

COLD CUCUMBER SOUP

·

This soup would probably be just as good in the winter, but it was born to be sipped, even slurped, on a hot summer evening.

2 medium cucumbers, peeled and cut into chunks	*1 quart buttermilk*
	½ teaspoon salt
1 small onion, chopped	*Freshly ground pepper to taste*
2 teaspoons snipped fresh dill	*3 to 4 radishes, very thinly sliced*

$\mathcal{P}$ut the cucumber chunks, onion, dill, and 1 cup of the buttermilk in a food processor or blender and process until smooth. Pour into a glass jar and add the rest of the buttermilk and the salt and pepper. Chill thoroughly. Shake before pouring into a serving bowl. Garnish with the radish slices.

WINTER TOMATO SOUP

■

Good to make in winter, when canned tomatoes are usually much tastier than their pale cousins in the fresh-produce department. Bring a box of garlic croutons or thin toasted bagel slices to serve with the soup.

4 tablespoons butter
1 cup chopped onion
1 cup diced celery
1 quart canned tomatoes in tomato puree (or one 28-ounce can)

1 quart beef broth (or two 13¾-ounce cans)
1 teaspoon sugar
Freshly ground pepper to taste
Dash of ground cloves

$\mathcal{I}$n a 4-quart pot, melt the butter and sauté the onion and celery until they are soft. Crush the tomatoes with your fingers (hold them down in the pot so they don't squirt) and add to the pot with their puree. Stir in the beef broth, sugar, pepper, and cloves. Simmer for at least 20 minutes. Serve hot.

CHILLED PEACH SOUP

·

The key to this soup is finding nice ripe peaches.

4 cups peeled and chopped ripe
  peaches (about 12 medium
  peaches)
1½ cups peach juice or nectar
1 tablespoon honey

2 tablespoons fresh lemon juice
1 cup sour cream or plain yogurt
½ teaspoon ground cinnamon
½ teaspoon freshly grated nutmeg
1 teaspoon vanilla

To peel fresh peaches more easily, first blanch them in boiling water for 2 to 3 minutes. Combine the chopped peaches and the remaining ingredients in a blender (do this in 2 batches, unless you have an industrial-size blender). Pour into a large glass jar and chill for 2 hours or more. To serve, pour into a pitcher and stir well.

HEARTY SOUPS (SPOONS NEEDED)

VEGETARIAN CHILI

•

2 cups (1 pound) dry kidney
  beans
2 quarts water
One 28-ounce can crushed
  tomatoes
3 tablespoons vegetable oil
½ cup TVP (textured vegetable
  protein—available in health food
  stores)
2 cups chopped onion
5 or 6 cloves garlic, minced

1 large green pepper, seeded and
  chopped
½ cup chopped carrots
2 teaspoons chili powder (or to
  your taste)
1 teaspoon ground cumin
1 teaspoon salt
Dash of cayenne pepper
Grated Cheddar cheese for
  topping

Wash and soak the kidney beans overnight in a heavy 4-quart soup pot. Pour off the water and add the 2 quarts fresh water. Bring to a boil, lower the heat, cover, and simmer until the beans are soft (about 1½ hours). Heat the oil in a heavy frying pan and sauté the TVP, onion, garlic, green pepper, carrots, chili powder, and cumin until the vegetables are tender. Add to the beans, adding more water if necessary. Add the salt and cayenne to taste. Simmer for another 30 minutes, stirring frequently. Serve hot with a side dish of grated cheese for topping.

CURRIED SPLIT PEA SOUP

·

2 cups (1 pound) yellow or green
  split peas, washed
1 quart chicken broth
1 quart water
2 to 3 tablespoons vegetable oil
1 cup chopped onion

4 to 5 cloves garlic, minced
2 tablespoons minced ginger
2 to 3 teaspoons good curry
  powder (or to your taste)
½ teaspoon salt
1½ cups chopped kale or spinach

In a 4-quart soup pot, cook the peas in the broth and water over low heat for about 45 minutes, stirring occasionally. Heat the oil in a heavy frying pan, then sauté the onion, garlic, and ginger until tender. Sprinkle the curry powder over the onion mixture and sauté for several minutes to mellow the flavors. Add the mixture in the frying pan to the cooked peas. Add the salt and kale or spinach and simmer, covered, for another 20 minutes. Stir frequently to be sure the soup doesn't stick. Serve hot with chapati or pita bread.

FRESH CORN AND GINGER SOUP

·

4 ears freshest sweet corn
1 small onion, finely chopped
1 small zucchini, chopped
1 sweet red pepper, seeded and
  chopped
1 to 2 tablespoons minced ginger

¼ cup butter
1 quart chicken broth
½ teaspoon ground cumin
Salt and pepper to taste
½ cup light cream

Shuck the corn. With a very sharp knife, cut the kernels off the cobs (don't cut too deeply or you will get too much of the cob). In a heavy 4-quart soup pot, combine the corn kernels and juices, onion, zucchini, red pepper, ginger, and butter. Cook gently over low heat until the vegetables are crisp-tender. Add the chicken broth and cumin and simmer gently for about 10 minutes. Add salt and pepper and adjust the seasonings. Just before serving, stir in the cream (do not let the cream boil).

Three

SALADS

·

Salads, more than any other type of food, lend themselves to extensive improvisation. Since most salads call for at least some, if not mostly, fresh ingredients, the availability (or lack thereof) of certain ingredients becomes a determining factor. Furthermore, with fresh ingredients one is more likely to vary quantities—you probably aren't going to use a cup of chopped peppers, but rather the whole pepper, or a whole stalk of celery. The specific proportions of the ingredients matter to some degree, but beyond that there is much room for experimentation. The salad becomes like a good jazz session—sometimes very intense, and sometimes laid back, but always with some specific emerging tone or flavor.

Therefore, while we encourage the concept of improvisation with any recipe in this book, nowhere is it meant more seriously than in this chapter. In fact, we'd be quite disappointed if we found that anyone followed one of these recipes to every detail!

On the other hand, if a group of jazz musicians started playing anything they wanted all at once, without regard to one another, the resulting cacophony would send listeners out of the room. If there is a bit of chopped cucumber in a salad, it's there for a reason, and it's got to work with all the other players. If each component of a salad doesn't contribute something harmonious to the flavor, then it shouldn't be there.

Therefore, what we've tried to do with each of these recipes is to set the tone for what the salad should be like. You take it from there.

A WORD ABOUT SALAD DRESSINGS

Most of these recipes include dressings, with which you can experiment in the same way as you do with the salad itself. There are of course so many different bottled dressings available in stores today. A few of these are good, some are okay, and most of them are—well, let's just say that they don't compare with what you can do yourself.

The secret to good salad dressing is the oil, which is the primary component. Oils pressed from a single source are better than blended oils, and generally you get what you pay for—the more expensive oils taste better. Extra-virgin (cold-pressed from high-grade olives) and virgin (first pressing)* olive oils, albeit expensive, are readily available. More exotic nut and seed oils may be hard to find, but probably worth exploring at some point. Unfortunately, the quality of oil doesn't have any influence over its shelf life. The finest oils can go stale or rancid in less than a month if not refrigerated.

Wine vinegar (red or white) or balsamic vinegar is preferable to white or cider vinegar for salad dressings. Wine vinegars provide a good base for making flavored vinegars: Add a specific herb, and allow it to steep for a few weeks.

When mixing a dressing, it is usually best to add the flavoring ingredients to the non-oil portion of the base and let the flavors mix before adding the oil.

---

* Contrary to popular belief, virgin olives are not the ones with the pimiento still intact.

And finally, getting back to the jazz analogy, fresh garlic is what provides the blue notes. It just isn't the same with the powdered stuff.

TIP Instead of laboriously peeling the garlic, just crush the clove with the bottom of a jar or coffee mug. The skin will slide right off the "meat" of the garlic.

NOTE Where it is appropriate, we have listed the ingredients for the dressing first. This is because in most cases the dressing can be prepared in advance.

CARROTS WITH ZUCCHINI VINAIGRETTE

—————

•

DRESSING
2 tablespoons tarragon vinegar
½ teaspoon Dijon mustard
¼ teaspoon sugar
¼ teaspoon salt

⅛ teaspoon pepper
1 teaspoon dried tarragon
¼ cup olive oil

2 pounds baby carrots
1 medium zucchini (about 1
  pound)

*P*repare the dressing and set aside. Set a couple of quarts of water to boil. Peel and trim the carrots and add them to the boiling water. Cook 5 to 10 minutes, depending on the size. Meanwhile, cut the zucchini across the diameter into thirds and then those thirds into julienne strips. A minute or two before you think the carrots will be tender, add the zucchini to the water. Drain, then rinse under cold water. Set on a paper or cloth towel to dry.

When the carrots and zucchini are dry, they may be tossed with the dressing until well coated.

BEET AND
RED ONION SALAD

·

2 pounds beets, trimmed and
  washed (about 8 beets)
2 whole cloves
2 whole allspice
1 bay leaf
Salt and pepper to taste

½ teaspoon sugar
2 teaspoons red wine vinegar
2 tablespoons chopped parsley
1 large red onion, peeled and
  thinly sliced into rings

*P*lace the beets in a saucepan and cover with water. Add the
cloves, allspice, and bay leaf. Bring to a boil and then simmer
for about 20 minutes or until the beets are cooked.

Remove the beets, slip the skins off as you run cold water over
them, and slice them. In a mixing bowl, toss the beets with the
remaining ingredients.

SHREDDED BEETS
WITH WALNUTS

·

1½ pounds beets (about 6 beets)
2 cups finely ground walnuts
2 cloves garlic, pressed
½ teaspoon salt

¼ cup red wine vinegar
2 tablespoons chopped fresh
parsley

*P*lace the beets in a saucepan and cover with water. Bring to a
boil and then simmer for about 20 minutes or until the beets
are cooked. Remove the beets and slip the skins off as you run cold
water over them. Grate the beets into a bowl, add the walnuts, and
mix well. Separately, mix the garlic, salt, and vinegar and then toss
with the beets. Sprinkle the parsley on top just before serving.

SEVEN-LAYER SALAD

■

from Celeste Hewson

THOMPSON STATION, TENNESSEE

½ head lettuce, chopped
½ cup chopped celery
½ cup chopped scallions
½ cup chopped green pepper
One 10-ounce package green peas,
 thawed, or fresh equivalent

2 hard-boiled eggs, sliced
1 cup mayonnaise (or ½ cup
 mayonnaise and ½ cup yogurt)
1 cup grated cheese
Bacon bits

Layer in the order given. Chill overnight.

COLESLAW

When Gordon's sister Celeste first moved from Maine to Tennessee, she naturally sought out various social groups within the community to become involved with. At one of the first meetings she attended, there were plans being made for a community supper. The most hotly debated topic was the coleslaw, which some folks insisted must be dressed with real mayonnaise, while others were just as adamant about using "salad dressing." Poppy seeds or no poppy seeds, pineapple or no pineapple, such "variables" were presented by their respective supporters as being indispensable to a proper slaw. Celeste, who is no slouch when it comes to making a decent coleslaw herself, decided she'd keep out of it altogether and offered to bring something else instead. Since coleslaw is, by literal definition, cabbage salad, there's no reason you can't do just about anything so long as you use your head, so to speak. Here are a few possibilities.

COLESLAW
·

DRESSING
1 cup mayonnaise
2 tablespoons vinegar (see page 58)
2 tablespoons sugar

1 teaspoon caraway seed
1 teaspoon celery seed
Salt and pepper to taste

1 head cabbage, coarsely grated
3 carrots, peeled and coarsely grated
3 stalks celery, finely chopped

7 to 10 radishes, thinly sliced
2 small or 1 large onion, finely chopped

Prepare the dressing, then mix into the vegetables. Chill before serving.

SWEET SLAW

•

DRESSING
¾ cup mayonnaise
1 tablespoon fresh lemon juice

Salt and pepper to taste
½ teaspoon ground cumin

½ small head green cabbage
½ small head purple cabbage
One 8-ounce can crushed
  pineapple, drained

½ cup raisins
½ cup sunflower seeds

*P*repare the dressing, then mix into the remaining ingredients.

CRANBERRY COLESLAW

•

¼ cup chopped cranberries
1 tablespoon honey
1 teaspoon celery seed
1 teaspoon vinegar or lemon juice

¼ cup mayonnaise
3 cups shredded cabbage
Salt to taste

*M*ix the cranberries, honey, and celery seed together and let set for about 15 minutes. Mix the vinegar or lemon juice and the mayonnaise and add to the cranberries. Pour all this over the cabbage and toss just enough to mix. Season with salt.

MERLE'S CAULIFLOWER COLESLAW

·

from Merle Peery

COLUMBIA, TENNESSEE

DRESSING
½ cup mayonnaise
½ teaspoon sugar

½ teaspoon vinegar
Cream for desired consistency

4 cups shredded cabbage
3 or 4 peeled carrots, grated
½ cup diced green pepper
4 scallions, diced

1 cup grated cauliflower
½ teaspoon celery seed
Salt and pepper to taste

Prepare the dressing, then mix the vegetables together. Toss with the dressing and then season with the celery seed and salt and pepper.

NOTE Certain "lite" mayonnaises seem to thicken instead of to thin with the addition of milk or cream. If you must use them, omit the cream.

FRESH GREEN BEAN SALAD

·

DRESSING
1 cup sugar
⅞ cup vinegar
½ cup olive oil

½ teaspoon salt
½ teaspoon pepper

8 cups cut-up green beans (in
  2-inch pieces)
One 8-ounce can sliced water
  chestnuts

1 medium red onion, sliced
4 ounces blue cheese, crumbled

Combine all the dressing ingredients in a saucepan and bring to a
boil. Meanwhile, steam the beans and then place in a bowl with
the water chestnuts and onion. Pour the hot dressing over the beans
and toss in the blue cheese. Chill before serving.

GREEN BEANS WITH RED ONION

·

DRESSING
1 tablespoon red wine vinegar
1 teaspoon Dijon mustard

3 tablespoons olive oil

1 pound green beans
½ cup chopped red onion

Salt and pepper to taste

Prepare the dressing. Add the vinegar to the mustard and whisk
in the oil. Set aside.

Trim and cut the beans into 2-inch lengths and steam until
slightly tender but still crisp. Drain, place in a bowl with the onion,
and toss with the dressing. Add salt and pepper. Cool to room
temperature before serving.

ITALIAN GREEN
BEAN SALAD

∎

DRESSING
1 clove garlic
1 teaspoon salt
1 tablespoon vinegar

1 tablespoon prepared mustard
¼ teaspoon pepper
3 tablespoons olive oil

2 pounds green beans
2 large ripe tomatoes, cut into
  wedges
½ cup ripe olives

1 (2-ounce) can flat anchovies,
  drained
½ cup freshly grated Parmesan
  cheese

℘repare the dressing. Crush the garlic into the salt. Add the vinegar, then remove the garlic. Add the mustard and pepper, then whisk or blend in the olive oil.

Cut the beans into 2-inch lengths and steam until tender. Drain and let set until reasonably dry, then toss with the dressing. Top with the remaining ingredients.

SPICY GREEN BEANS

∎

Polly Bannister, already a dear friend, became an even better friend when she served us this tasty bean salad.

DRESSING
1 tablespoon Dijon mustard
3 tablespoons lemon juice
¼ teaspoon cayenne pepper
1 teaspoon salt

4 tablespoons olive oil
1½ tablespoons mustard seeds
2 medium cloves garlic, minced

1 pound green beans, trimmed

*P*repare the dressing. Thoroughly mix the mustard, lemon juice, cayenne, and salt and set aside.

In a small (cast iron) skillet, heat the oil. When it is hot, add the mustard seeds and sauté until they start to pop. Then add the garlic and sauté until lightly browned. Beat the oil mixture with the lemon juice mixture into a creamy dressing.

Boil the green beans to crisp-tender, 3 to 5 minutes, and toss with the dressing. Refrigerate and serve cold.

VEGETABLE-BARLEY SALAD

•

DRESSING

½ cup olive oil	¾ teaspoon salt
½ cup lemon juice	½ teaspoon pepper
1 tablespoon sugar	

4 cups water	¼ cup chopped parsley
1½ cups quick-cooking barley	1 tablespoon chopped fresh mint
1 medium cucumber, chopped	or 1 teaspoon dried
1 sweet red or green pepper, cut	3 stalks celery, chopped
into strips	Fresh greens and tomato for
¼ cup chopped red onion	garnish

*P*repare the dressing and set aside. Boil the water and add the barley. Return to boiling, cover, and simmer. When the barley is done, about 10 to 12 minutes, remove, drain, and rinse with cold water.

Stir the barley together with the remaining ingredients, toss with the dressing, and chill for several hours. Garnish with fresh greens and chopped tomato.

SAFFRON RICE SALAD

·

DRESSING

2 cloves garlic, pressed
½ teaspoon salt
½ teaspoon pepper

4 tablespoons red wine vinegar
6 tablespoons olive oil
2 tablespoons sesame oil

3 cups water
1½ cups long-grain rice
  (uncooked)
½ teaspoon saffron threads,
  crushed and dissolved in 1
  tablespoon boiling water
½ sweet red pepper, thinly sliced
½ sweet green pepper, thinly
  sliced (toss the seeds in too—
  they're good)

1 ripe tomato, sliced and chopped
1 cup cooked chick peas
1 cup cooked green peas
⅓ cup pitted and sliced black
  olives
⅓ cup slivered almonds

Prepare the dressing. Mix the garlic, salt, and pepper into the vinegar. Whisk in the oil to blend. Set aside.

Bring the water to a boil and add the rice and saffron. Stir thoroughly to mix the saffron. When the water returns to a boil, cover and simmer until the liquid is absorbed, about 20 minutes. Meanwhile, prepare the remaining ingredients as needed, and when the rice is done, mix everything together. Toss with the dressing. Serve at room temperature or slightly chilled.

COLD LENTIL SALAD

■

This recipe is from Carolyn Edwards of Fitzwilliam, New Hampshire. She says she's had it in her handwritten recipe book for about twenty years.

DRESSING

¼ cup wine vinegar or lemon juice
¼ teaspoon sugar
1 clove garlic, finely chopped

½ teaspoon Worcestershire sauce
A few drops of Tabasco sauce
Salt and pepper to taste
⅔ cup olive oil

1 pound dry lentils
1 bay leaf
1½ teaspoons salt

2 onions, each stuck with 2 whole cloves

½ cup finely chopped scallions
3 tablespoons chopped parsley
3 hard-boiled eggs, quartered or sliced

1½ cups (about 6 ounces) thinly sliced pepperoni (optional)

Prepare the dressing in advance and set aside or prepare while the lentils are cooking.

Put the lentils, seasonings, and onions into a heavy saucepan with 5 cups of water. Bring to a boil and simmer for 30 minutes. Drain off the excess liquid. Remove the onions and bay leaf.

Pour the dressing over the hot lentils. Toss gently. Chill overnight or for several hours.

Shortly before serving, mix the scallions and parsley into the lentils. Top with the eggs and pepperoni if desired. Keep chilled until ready to serve.

CRACKED WHEAT AND TOMATO SALAD

·

1 cup fine bulgur
2 cups cold water
3 tablespoons tomato paste
½ cup tomato sauce
1 medium fresh tomato, chopped
 into cubes
6 to 8 scallions, minced

½ cup chopped parsley
¾ cup olive oil
¼ cup red wine vinegar
¼ cup lemon juice
½ teaspoon salt
A few shakes of pepper
Pinch of cayenne pepper

Place the bulgur in a bowl and stir in the water. Let it set for an hour or until the water is absorbed. Add the tomato paste and sauce and stir until combined. Stir in the fresh tomato, scallions, parsley, and oil. Add the remaining ingredients and stir just enough to mix.

MINTED BULGUR WITH PEAS

·

1 cup coarse bulgur (not cracked)
2 cups shelled fresh or frozen peas
1 tablespoon chopped fresh basil
4 tablespoons chopped fresh
 parsley
4 tablespoons chopped fresh mint

3 scallions, sliced thin
2 tablespoons lemon juice
Salt and pepper to taste
1 cup plain yogurt
¼ cup sliced almonds

Cover the bulgur with hot water and let stand for 30 minutes. Drain and press out the excess water. Blanch the fresh peas in boiling water for 1 minute. (If using frozen peas, thaw but do not cook.)

Combine the bulgur, peas, and everything else except the yogurt and almonds. After everything is well mixed, stir in the yogurt. Top with the almonds.

TABOULI

■

½ cup fine bulgur, soaked in hot
  water for 1 hour
4 stalks celery
1 large green pepper
4 scallions
2 cloves garlic, sliced

2 medium cucumbers, peeled
1 cup loose parsley sprigs
½ cup mint leaves
½ cup olive oil
¼ cup fresh lemon juice
1 ripe tomato, finely diced

*D*rain the bulgur, press out the excess water, and place in a large bowl. Cut the celery, green pepper, and scallions into large pieces and whirl with the garlic in a food processor until finely chopped. Add to the bulgur. Place the cucumbers, parsley, and mint leaves in the food processor and pulse until chopped (do not overdo it or the cucumber will be pureed). Add to the mixture in the bowl. Pour the olive oil and lemon juice over all and toss to mix. Sprinkle the diced tomato on top and refrigerate for at least 1 hour before serving.

POTATOES

On the morning of our wedding day I woke up at four-thirty. I gazed out the window and in the early dawn light studied our first garden—a motley collection of rocks and weeds and a few seedlings in a rough rectangle of most ambitious dimension. In future years the garden would be better.

It is important when one is arriving at certain milestones in life to feel that one's house is in order, that there aren't things left undone. As I surveyed the incomplete garden, I realized that I still had a large bag of seed potatoes in the cellar. It wasn't exactly that I'd forgotten them. The spring had been unusually wet, as was the garden itself, and when I might have planted them I was too busy with other projects. But now, suddenly, here I was on June 21, about to get married, and I hadn't planted my potatoes yet.

The task now revealed, I headed out to the garden through a herd of black flies and set those spuds in. Now I was ready to get married to Susan.

A few weeks passed, and we could see that there must be some new potatoes in the ground. We would be content to let most of them grow to full size, but we needed to have just a taste of the fruits of my nuptial morning's labor. I brought just a handful of potatoes in, set a pot of water to boil, wiped the dirt off their tender skins, and approached the first one with a knife to cut it in half. I had just barely set the knife into it when I heard a beautiful, rich, cracking sound—like ice cracking on a pond, or like an ash log being split on a sub-zero day. It was that potato, full of life all the way through. I cut up the others (they sang too) and cooked them, then served them up with lots of butter, garlic, and parsley. You know the rest.

Sometime later Susan received a box in the mail—obviously a promotional kit from a food company. We opened the sturdy box and saw a layer of gold-foil-wrapped spheres, each set in a foam-padded cubicle. Golden apples? Exotic pears? Forbidden fruits from a tropical island? It turned out to be potatoes—a special kind with a slightly yellow meat that was supposed to give a buttery look to it. The accompanying literature went out of its way to establish the fact that the lowly image of the potato was not really representative of what potatoes were really all about, especially these potatoes.

Little did those marketing people know that we had already accorded to the humble potato a dignity above kings and queens.

—G.P.

RED-SKINNED POTATO AND ARTICHOKE SALAD

·

Gordon's father, Russell, and his wife, Merle, live in Columbia, Tennessee. Merle sent us this recipe. Of course, it's hard to go wrong with artichoke hearts, but the rest of it is pretty good too.

DRESSING

2 tablespoons lemon juice
2 tablespoons spicy mustard
Salt and pepper to taste

¾ teaspoon dried oregano
⅓ cup olive oil

1½ pounds unpeeled small red
  potatoes
One 6-ounce jar marinated
  artichoke hearts, drained

2 hard-boiled eggs, quartered
1 small sweet red pepper, coarsely
  diced
½ cup pitted and sliced ripe olives

3 scallions, sliced

*P*repare the dressing. Combine the lemon juice, mustard, salt and pepper, and oregano. Shake or whisk to combine. Add the oil and shake or blend again. Set aside.

Cook the potatoes until just tender, 15 to 20 minutes. Drain and transfer to a large bowl. Pour the dressing over while the potatoes are still warm, toss lightly, and chill. Add the remaining ingredients and toss gently.

S A L A D   N I Ç O I S E

·

DRESSING

1 clove garlic
1 teaspoon salt
1 tablespoon vinegar

¼ teaspoon pepper
1 tablespoon prepared mustard
3 tablespoons olive oil

8 new red potatoes*
2 cloves garlic
½ teaspoon salt
2 pounds green beans, cut and
 steamed lightly
1½ pounds asparagus, steamed
 lightly
20 cherry tomatoes, washed and
 halved
2 carrots, diced

1 purple onion, thinly sliced
½ cup pitted whole black olives
¼ cup chopped parsley
Salt and pepper to taste
One 12-ounce can tuna, drained
6 hard-boiled eggs, quartered
One 2-ounce can anchovies,
 drained
¼ cup chopped fresh dill

*P*repare the dressing and set aside.
 Cook the potatoes in boiling salted water for about 10 minutes
or until just tender. Drain. Meanwhile, crush the garlic into the salt
in the bottom of a large bowl and rub the entire inside of the bowl
with the garlic. When the potatoes are cool enough to work, quarter
them and set in the bowl. Combine all the vegetables, season with
salt and pepper, and toss with the vinaigrette or French dressing.

 Artistically place the tuna on the top, surrounded by the eggs and
anchovies. Sprinkle with the dill.

* New red potatoes will be about 1 to 1½ inches in diameter. If unavailable, select the
smallest red potatoes you can find, or quarter larger ones before cooking.

POTATO SALAD
CAESAR STYLE

■

DRESSING

2 cloves garlic, sliced
½ cup olive oil
1 teaspoon salt
¼ cup grated Parmesan cheese

¼ cup lemon juice
¼ teaspoon pepper
¼ teaspoon dry mustard
1 tablespoon Worcestershire sauce

3 pounds potatoes, cut into chunks
  and cooked
5 bacon slices, fried and crumbled

1 medium onion, diced
¼ cup chopped parsley
2 hard-boiled eggs, sliced

*P*repare the dressing. Steep the garlic in the olive oil overnight. Mix all the other ingredients together and then blend with the oil. Set aside.

Mix together all the salad ingredients except the eggs. Toss gently with the dressing. Top with the egg slices.

POTATO SALAD
WITH PESTO

•

We made so much pesto one year that we had to put it on nearly everything to use it up. That suited us fine.

PESTO

4 cups loosely packed fresh basil leaves

4 cloves garlic (or more if you're into it)

¾ cup olive oil

½ cup pine nuts or walnuts

½ cup grated Parmesan cheese

3 pounds potatoes, cut into bite-sized squares and cooked just until tender

½ green pepper, diced

1 carrot, grated

6 to 8 cherry tomatoes, halved

If you have a food processor, put all the pesto ingredients into it and process until well blended. If you don't have a food processor, chop everything as finely as you can and mix together.

Toss the pesto with the potatoes, green pepper, and carrot. If the pesto seems too thick, add some more olive oil. Top with the tomatoes.

SIMPLE POTATOES WITH BASIL

·

One of the nicest ways to enjoy potatoes is in this uncomplicated style. It tastes great when the potatoes are still warm, but it is fine cold too. Make some for yourself for dinner and bring the leftovers to a potluck.

*1 cup loosely packed fresh basil
leaves*
*3 pounds potatoes, cut into bite-
sized squares and cooked just
until tender*

¼ cup olive oil
1 tablespoon lemon juice
Salt and pepper to taste

Coarsely chop the basil when the potatoes are almost done. When cooked, drain the potatoes, put into a large bowl, and toss with the basil and oil. Add the lemon juice and toss lightly again. Season with salt and pepper.

HUNAN BEAN CURD WITH THOUSAND-YEAR-EGG SALAD

■

from Julie and Dan Brody

NEWTON, MASSACHUSETTS

HOT AND SOUR DRESSING

3 tablespoons soy sauce

2 tablespoons Chinese sesame oil

1 teaspoon brown sugar

1 tablespoon minced fresh ginger

1 tablespoon minced scallions

1 to 2 cups chicken broth

4 tablespoons vinegar

1 tablespoon Chinese hot pepper oil (or to taste)

½ teaspoon pepper

2 tablespoons vegetable oil

3 cloves garlic, minced

1 tablespoon white wine or sherry

1 tablespoon minced fresh coriander leaves (cilantro)

4 thousand-year eggs, shelled

2 to 3 squares bean curd (tofu)

1 tablespoon Chinese sesame oil

1 tablespoon finely minced scallions

Mix all the dressing ingredients in a small bowl. Cut the bean curd and the thousand-year eggs into ½-inch cubes. Toss them together gently in a large bowl. Pour the dressing over the salad and again toss gently. Sprinkle the sesame oil and the scallions on top for garnish. Serve chilled or at room temperature.

Thousand-year eggs are available at Chinese markets. They are really about two to three months old. They're made from chicken eggs preserved in a mixture of salt and rice-straw ashes, then coated in black clay. To shell the eggs, tap the hard clay against the counter and peel off. The egg white inside will be brown with shiny spots and the yolk will be dark green.

This recipe is modified from one we got from Henry Chung on Chinese New Year's at a cooking demonstration at San Francisco's Macy's. Henry Chung runs the Hunan Restaurant in San Francisco, which started out as a hole-in-the-wall but became famous when it was mentioned in The New Yorker (much to the distress of those of us who had discovered it before they did).

Believe it or not, this has become a traditional Fourth of July potluck picnic dish in our family. It's great with fried chicken. We used to take it down to the river in Austin, Texas, where we would join other families waiting for the fireworks. It makes you feel that you're at a very special, sophisticated, and grown-up occasion even if there are kids crawling all over you.

If you aren't up for the bean curd and thousand-year eggs, the dressing can be tossed with cold cooked buckwheat noodles and matchstick vegetables instead. Dan always makes this version for the Zervas School Spring Fair potluck lunch table.

—J.B.

GUACAMOLE CHICKEN SALAD

■

½ cup mayonnaise
2 tablespoons lemon juice
½ teaspoon salt
3 cups chopped cooked chicken

1 cup chopped celery
2 cloves garlic, pressed
1 medium tomato, chopped
1 avocado, diced

Combine the mayonnaise with the lemon juice and salt. Combine all the other ingredients, then dress with the mayonnaise mixture, mixing as little as possible to cover everything. Chill before serving.

TRADE WINDS SALAD

■

2 tablespoons butter
¼ cup dark-brown sugar
1 cup cubed ham
8 ounces large pasta shells,
  cooked, rinsed, and drained
One 8-ounce can pineapple
  chunks, drained and juice
  reserved

½ cup halved grapes
½ cup chopped apple
1 cup cubed Cheddar cheese
¼ cup mayonnaise
¼ cup sour cream
½ teaspoon salt

In a medium skillet, melt the butter and brown sugar together. Add the ham and cook until it is brown. Let this cool. In a large bowl, combine the ham, shells, pineapple, grapes, apple, and cheese. In a small bowl, combine the mayonnaise, sour cream, 2 tablespoons of the pineapple juice (you may drink the rest), and salt. Toss everything together and chill.

CURRIED CHICKEN SALAD

▪

This recipe was sent to us by Gordon's aunt, Sally Spiegel. She in turn got it from her friend Jean Wargo.

3 cups (or more) cubed cooked
  chicken
1 cup chopped celery
1 teaspoon salt
1 tablespoon lemon juice
1 cup halved green grapes
One 8-ounce can sliced water
  chestnuts, drained

One 8-ounce can pineapple
  chunks, drained
1 cup mayonnaise
2 teaspoons curry powder
1 tablespoon soy sauce
1 cup toasted slivered almonds

Mix together everything, up to and including the pineapple chunks. Then mix the mayonnaise, curry powder, and soy sauce and toss this with the chicken mixture. Refrigerate overnight or until chilled. Sprinkle with the almonds before serving.

WHITE BEAN AND TUNA SALAD

■

DRESSING

1 tablespoon lemon juice
¼ teaspoon salt

¼ teaspoon pepper
¼ cup olive oil

1 cup navy beans
2 scallions, chopped
1 tablespoon chopped pimiento

2 tablespoons minced parsley
One 7-ounce can tuna packed in
  olive oil

*P*repare the dressing and set aside. Put the beans in 2 quarts of water and bring to a boil. After they have boiled briskly for 2 minutes, remove from the heat and let stand for 1 hour. Drain, place in 2 quarts of fresh water, and bring to a boil again. As soon as a boil is reached, cover and simmer for 1½ hours or until tender. Drain. Pour the dressing over the beans while they are still warm and add the remaining ingredients. Mix everything together gently. Chill before serving.

NEW DELHI TUNA

■

One 12-ounce can tuna, drained
1 cup chopped apple
¼ cup chopped cauliflower
½ cup chopped celery
4 or 5 scallions, chopped
¼ cup golden raisins

¼ cup slivered almonds
¾ cup mayonnaise
2 tablespoons ground turmeric
1 teaspoon curry powder
1 tablespoon lemon juice

*J*ust mix it all together!

PINEAPPLE TUNA

■

One 12-ounce can tuna
1 cup chopped celery
One 8-ounce can crushed
  pineapple, drained
¼ cup diced green pepper
1 teaspoon ground ginger or
  2 teaspoons finely diced
  fresh ginger

Salt to taste
Dash of pepper
½ cup mayonnaise

*F*ollow the detailed mixing instructions provided in the previous recipe.

SALMON-RICE SALAD

■

This recipe provides a good escape for leftover rice.

One 15½-ounce can sockeye
  salmon, drained and flaked
1 cup cooked white rice
1 hard-boiled egg, chopped
2 tablespoons lemon juice

2 tablespoons mayonnaise
2 teaspoons finely diced onion
¼ teaspoon salt
⅛ teaspoon pepper
¼ cup raw or cooked peas

*M*ix all the ingredients, leaving the peas out until everything else is well combined. Serve.

MACARONI AND SHRIMP SALAD

■

DRESSING
¼ cup olive oil
1½ tablespoons lemon juice
2 cloves garlic, minced

½ teaspoon salt
¼ teaspoon pepper

1 pound rotini or other macaroni
Olive oil
1 pound small–medium shrimp
4 scallions, sliced on the diagonal

¼ cup sliced pimiento-stuffed
  green olives
12 cherry tomatoes, halved
¼ cup chopped parsley

*B*lend the dressing ingredients together and put into a sealable
container. Refrigerate. Cook the pasta according to package
directions. Drain, toss with a sprinkling of olive oil, and set aside.
Peel and wash the shrimp if necessary, and cook for 5 minutes or
less in boiling water. Drain and let cool.

Combine the shrimp, pasta, scallions, and olives. Just before serving, toss with the dressing. Garnish with the tomatoes and parsley.

SHRIMP SUMMER SALAD

•

from Julie Rohr

NELSON, NEW HAMPSHIRE

DRESSING

1 tablespoon soy sauce
2 teaspoons curry powder
½ teaspoon sugar

3 tablespoons vinegar
½ cup olive oil
½ teaspoon celery seed

One 12-ounce package long-grain
  and wild rice mix
1 cup diced celery
½ cup diced carrots

¼ cup diced onion
1 pound medium shrimp
¼ cup slivered almonds

*B*lend the dressing ingredients together and set aside. Cook the
rice according to package directions. Sauté the celery, carrots,
and onion. Peel and wash the shrimp if necessary and cook for 5
minutes or less in boiling water. Drain. When the rice is done,
combine with the vegetables and shrimp. Toss with the dressing.
Chill, and garnish with the almonds.

Four

RICE AND BEAN

DISHES

■

The well-appointed potluck table is bound to have beans and rice in some form, separately or in combination. They are not only complementary proteins (only one reason why Red Beans and Rice, page 97, is a classic) but complementary tastes. We have of late been using Texas-grown basmati rice (called Texmati) almost exclusively. It smells like popcorn while cooking and has a sweet, nutty taste. It also keeps its integrity in salads and pilafs.

CREOLE RICE

■

1½ cups rice (uncooked).
6 tablespoons butter
½ teaspoon salt
Ground black pepper to taste

1 cup pitted black Greek olives
1 cup loose parsley sprigs
2 large cloves garlic

Cook the rice until tender according to your usual method. Place the rice in a baking dish, toss with 2 tablespoons of the butter, season with the salt and pepper, and place in a preheated oven at 200°F to dry a bit. Toss occasionally. While the rice dries, pit the olives and set aside. Chop the parsley and garlic together until both are finely minced. Mix the olives, parsley-garlic combination, and remaining 4 tablespoons of butter into the rice. Serve warm.

TASTY RICE-PECAN PILAF

■

1½ cups brown rice (uncooked)
3 cups boiling water
2 cubes of chicken bouillon
2 tablespoons soy sauce
2 bunches scallions, chopped

1 pound mushrooms, sliced
Vegetable oil
½ cup coarsely chopped pecans
1 cup frozen peas

Over low heat, cook the rice in the water with the bouillon and soy sauce for 50 to 60 minutes or until the water is completely absorbed. Stir-fry the scallions and mushrooms in 1 tablespoon each vegetable oil and water. When the rice is tender, add the cooked vegetables, nuts, and frozen peas. The peas will thaw and the pilaf will be ready to serve in about 10 minutes.

THREE-GRAIN PILAF

■

1/4 cup butter
1/3 cup chopped almonds or
  walnuts
1 large onion, chopped
1 large carrot, finely diced
1 clove garlic, pressed
1/3 cup chopped parsley
1/3 cup barley

1/3 cup brown rice (uncooked)
1/3 cup bulgur wheat
2 1/2 cups chicken broth
1/4 cup dry sherry or water
3/4 teaspoon dried basil
3/4 teaspoon dried oregano
Salt and pepper to taste

In a 3-quart pot, melt the butter over medium heat. Add the nuts and stir until lightly toasted. Remove with a slotted spoon and set aside. Increase the heat and add the onion, carrot, garlic, and parsley. Cook, stirring frequently, until the onion is translucent. Add the barley, rice, and bulgur. Cook, stirring, until lightly browned. Add the broth, sherry or water, basil, and oregano. Bring to a boil, then reduce the heat. Cover and simmer until the liquid is absorbed, approximately 45 minutes. Remove from the heat and let stand, covered, for 10 minutes. Add salt and pepper. Garnish with the toasted nuts.

LEMON-DATE PILAF

•

3 tablespoons butter
¾ cup long-grain white rice
  (uncooked)
⅔ cup broken vermicelli
1⅓ cups chicken broth
½ cup sherry or water
1 bay leaf

1 cup chopped dates
½ cup toasted pecans
⅓ cup sliced scallions
¼ cup chopped parsley
1 teaspoon grated lemon peel
Salt and pepper to taste

In a large skillet, melt the butter. Add the rice and vermicelli. Sauté over medium heat until lightly browned. Stir in the broth, sherry or water, and bay leaf. Cover. Cook over low heat until the rice is tender and the liquid absorbed, about 15 minutes. Remove the bay leaf. Stir in the dates, pecans, scallions, parsley, and lemon peel. Season with salt and pepper.

CALIFORNIA SPICY RICE

•

2 cups water
1 cup long-grain rice (uncooked)
1 tablespoon liquid bouillon or
  3 cubes (chicken, beef, or
  vegetable)
1 pint sour cream

One 4-ounce can chopped green
  chilies
½ cup chopped sweet red pepper
⅛ teaspoon pepper
1½ cups shredded Colby cheese

Bring the water to a boil and add the rice and bouillon. Reduce the heat and cook the rice until tender. When it is done, add all the ingredients except the cheese and mix thoroughly. Put into a 1½-quart casserole dish and bake in a preheated oven at 350°F for 20 minutes (longer if the rice has cooled). Top with the cheese and bake for 5 more minutes or enough to let the cheese melt into the casserole.

ARMENIAN RICE-AND-MUSSEL PILAF

•

Two 10-ounce cans (or fresh equivalent) mussels, in their liquor
½ cup tomato sauce
¼ cup olive oil
2 cups coarsely chopped onion
1 teaspoon salt
2 teaspoons sugar
½ cup chopped fresh parsley
½ cup chopped fresh dill
½ teaspoon ground nutmeg
½ teaspoon ground cinnamon
1 cup long-grain rice (uncooked)
½ cup dried currants or raisins
½ cup pine nuts
Juice of 1 lemon
Lettuce leaves, dill sprigs, and lemon wedges for garnish

Drain the mussels through a sieve, reserving the liquor. Set the mussels aside. Pour the mussel liquor into a 2-cup measure. Add the tomato sauce and enough water to complete the 2 cups.

Heat the olive oil in a large skillet. Add the onion and sauté, stirring frequently, until transparent but not browned. Stir in the salt, sugar, parsley, dill, nutmeg, and cinnamon.

Add the rice, the mussels, 2 cups of the liquid, the currants or raisins, and the pine nuts to the skillet; stir until well mixed. Bring to a boil; cover and reduce the heat. Cook for 30 minutes or until the rice is tender. Stir in the lemon juice, remove the skillet from the heat, and let cool, covered, to room temperature.

Bring to the potluck in a sealed container and then set it out on a platter with the garnish.

C O W B O Y   B E A N S

■

Merle Peery, Gordon's stepmother, sent this recipe up from Tennessee. It's a good antidote to molasses-sweetened baked beans.

1 pound dry pinto or red beans
6 cups water
2 medium onions, thinly sliced
2 large cloves garlic, chopped
1 small bay leaf
½ pound salt pork or smoked
   ham, or 6 slices bacon
1 tablespoon margarine

One 16-ounce can whole tomatoes
½ cup chopped green pepper
2 tablespoons brown sugar
2 teaspoons chili powder
½ teaspoon dry mustard
½ teaspoon ground cumin
Salt to taste

Wash the beans, drain, and soak overnight in the 6 cups water, or bring to a boil, simmer for 2 minutes, then remove from the heat and set aside for 1 hour. Do not drain. Stir in the onions, garlic, and bay leaf. If using salt pork, wash thoroughly and score (cut ham or bacon into ½-inch slices). Add the meat to the beans and bring rapidly to boiling. Add the margarine to prevent foaming. Cover and simmer for about 1½ hours. Stir in the tomatoes, green pepper, sugar, chili powder, mustard, and cumin. Return to a boil. Add salt. Simmer, covered, for several hours longer, stirring occasionally. Add water if needed: There should be enough liquid to make a medium-thick sauce.

NEW ENGLAND BAKED BEANS

•

Every New England cook has his or her definitive way of making baked beans. We don't know if our way is exactly definitive, but these beans are good, especially when accompanied by something tart (like pickles) and a chunk of warm brown bread or corn bread.

1 pound dry beans of choice
  (yellow-eye, Jacob's cattle, or
  soldier is what we'd pick)
½ pound salt pork
2 teaspoons salt (or more to taste)

⅓ cup molasses
2 teaspoons Coleman's dry
  mustard
1 peeled whole onion studded with
  5 or 6 cloves

Wash the beans and soak overnight in ample water. (A quicker way is to wash the beans, place in a heavy kettle with water to cover plus an inch more, and bring to a quick boil. Simmer for 2 minutes, cover, and remove from the heat. Let set for 1 hour. This has the same effect as soaking overnight.) Drain the water if it looks unappealing. Return the beans to the pot, add fresh water to cover, and parboil the beans until the skins burst when you blow on them. Meanwhile, wash the salt pork and score deeply. Place the beans and their liquid in a bean pot or heavy casserole. Push the salt pork down into the center. Add the salt, molasses, and mustard. Submerge the onion in the beans. Add boiling water if necessary to cover. Bake, covered, in a preheated oven at 275°F for several hours, replacing the water as it boils away. Remove the cover about a half hour before serving to let the top brown.

BAKED BEANS WITH CUMIN

———
•

This is an unsweetened type of baked bean.

1 pound dry white beans
2 onions, chopped
6 cloves garlic, minced
2 tablespoons olive oil

1 teaspoon salt
2 teaspoons ground cumin
½ teaspoon cayenne pepper
Ground black pepper to taste

Soak the beans overnight, or simmer as described in New England Baked Beans (see page 93). Place the soaked beans in water to cover and simmer gently until the bean skins break when you blow on them. Pour the beans and their liquid into a 4-quart casserole. In a heavy skillet, sauté the onions and garlic in the olive oil until tender. Add to the beans. Stir in the salt, cumin, cayenne, and black pepper. Add boiling water to cover. Bake, covered, for 1½ to 2 hours, until the beans are tender. Adjust the seasonings. Serve warm.

LENTIL-MUSHROOM CURRY

———
•

This is good warm or at room temperature. Don't omit the dollop of yogurt and sprinkling of scallions on each serving.

2 cups lentils
5 to 6 cups water
1 teaspoon salt
4 tablespoons olive oil
5 medium onions, chopped
1 pound mushrooms, sliced

2 to 3 teaspoons curry powder
  (or to taste)
2 cups plain yogurt
2 cups chopped scallions (green
  parts only)

ash the lentils and place in a heavy saucepan. Cook in 5 to 6 cups water at a simmer until the lentils are tender, about 40 minutes. Most of the water will have been absorbed. Add the salt and set aside. In a heavy skillet, heat the oil and sauté the onions, mushrooms, and curry powder. Combine the lentils with the onion mixture in a 2-quart baking dish. Bake, covered, in a preheated oven at 350°F for about 25 minutes. Top each serving with a spoonful of yogurt and a garnish of the scallions.

LENTIL-EGGPLANT
CASSEROLE
■

6 tablespoons butter
4 cups cubed eggplant (1 medium eggplant)
1 cup chopped onion
1 cup chopped celery
2 cups drained cooked lentils
1½ cups chopped ripe tomatoes with their juice (or canned equivalent)
½ teaspoon salt
Ground black pepper to taste
1 teaspoon dried oregano
¼ cup chopped basil
¼ cup chopped parsley
3 slices bread, made into crumbs (about 1½ cups fresh crumbs)
1 cup grated Cheddar cheese

elt the butter in a heavy skillet and sauté the eggplant, onion, and celery for several minutes, until crisp-tender. Stir in the lentils, tomatoes, salt, pepper, oregano, basil, and parsley, and heat through. Add ½ cup of the bread crumbs. Turn into a shallow 2-quart baking dish. Mix the remaining crumbs with the cheese and sprinkle over the top. Bake, uncovered, in a preheated oven at 350°F for about 30 minutes, until the crumbs are golden.

ITALIAN BEAN CASSEROLE

1 pound large dry white beans
 (marrows, white kidney, or
 Great Northern)
¼ cup olive oil
1 cup chopped onion
3 cloves garlic, minced
1 cup chopped celery
2 tablespoons chopped parsley
½ teaspoon dried thyme or
 2 teaspoons chopped fresh thyme

½ teaspoon dried basil or
 2 teaspoons chopped fresh basil
Ground black pepper to taste
1 cup skinned and chopped fresh
 tomatoes
Grated Parmesan or Romano
 cheese

𝒲ash the beans and soak overnight in water to cover, or use the quick method described in New England Baked Beans (see page 93). Drain and replace with fresh water if the water looks unappealing. Bring the beans to a boil, then simmer until tender, adding water as needed. Drain the beans, reserving the liquid. In a heavy skillet, heat the oil and sauté the onion, garlic, and celery. Add the parsley, thyme, basil, pepper, and tomatoes. Add the bean liquid and bring to a boil. Add to the beans and place in a 2-quart casserole. Cover and bake in a preheated oven at 350°F for 1 hour. Remove the cover, dust generously with grated cheese, and return to the oven briefly. Serve hot with additional cheese on the side.

If the casserole is to be reheated, omit the cheese until the casserole is rewarmed.

RED BEANS AND RICE

·

Although this dish is most commonly associated with New Orleans (where it's called Louisiana Turkey), every town in the Southland, from the Caribbean to California, has its own version. Here's an easy way to do it, using canned beans. (It's okay to start from scratch and cook your own, of course.)

2 tablespoons corn oil
1 large onion, finely chopped
2 stalks celery, finely chopped
1 large green pepper, finely
  chopped
3 cloves garlic, minced
One 16-ounce can kidney beans,
  drained, or 2 cups cooked
¼ cup chopped parsley

1 to 2 teaspoons salt
1 teaspoon dried thyme
½ teaspoon ground cumin
Tabasco sauce to taste
Worcestershire sauce to taste
4 ounces cooked smoked ham,
  finely diced
1 cup rice (uncooked)
2½ cups chicken broth or water

Heat the oil in a large, heavy skillet and sauté the onion, celery, green pepper, and garlic until tender, about 5 minutes. In a bean pot or heavy casserole, combine the sautéed vegetables with the kidney beans, parsley, salt, thyme, cumin, Tabasco, Worcestershire, ham, rice, and broth or water. Stir to combine. Cover and bake for at least 1 hour, until the rice is tender and the liquid is absorbed.

Five

P A S T A

■

A potluck supper would hardly be complete without the presence of at least one pasta dish. One friend of ours regularly arrives at potluck suppers with a box of spaghetti and a jar of pesto. He begs a pot, stove top, and serving dish and produces a simple but tasty and popular contribution to the meal.

Pasta is usually a sure hit with children, too, who otherwise might be forced to subsist on brownies.

For recipes calling for spaghetti, we recommend breaking it in half before cooking. This will make it easier to serve.

GORDON'S TOMATO SAUCE

■

1/3 cup olive oil
1 small-medium onion, diced
3 cloves garlic, pressed
1/4 cup diced green pepper
1 teaspoon dried basil
1 teaspoon dried oregano
1/4 teaspoon dried thyme
One 28-ounce can crushed
  tomatoes

One 6-ounce can tomato paste
1/4 cup red wine
1 teaspoon baking soda
1 tablespoon honey
Splash of red wine, about 2
  tablespoons
1/2 teaspoon salt
1/4 teaspoon pepper

Heat the oil in a 2-quart saucepan and sauté the onion, garlic, green pepper, basil, oregano, and thyme. When the onion is translucent, add the tomatoes and paste. Stir to mix. Sprinkle the baking soda over the sauce, then stir in. Add the honey, wine, salt, and pepper, and simmer for at least 30 minutes.

PASTA AND PEAS

—————
■

from Carol Thomas Downing

BALTIMORE, MARYLAND
—————————————————

Carol has hosted Gordon's contra dance band on several occasions when they were playing in Baltimore and has proved her culinary talents many times over. (Actually, Carol, we're still not quite convinced, so I guess we'll have to visit you again when we're in town.)

SAUCE

One 4-ounce jar diced pimiento	*4 teaspoons chili powder*
½ cup plain yogurt	*2 cloves garlic, pressed*
½ cup olive oil	*½ teaspoon cayenne pepper*
3 tablespoons lime or lemon juice	*1 small red onion, finely diced*

1 pound rotini, cooked al dente and rinsed	*Two 1-pound cans chick-peas, drained*
1 tablespoon olive oil	*One 1-pound can pitted black olives, sliced in half*
1 pound frozen green peas, thawed	

Mix or blend the sauce ingredients together. Toss the pasta and the remaining ingredients together in a large bowl. Pour the sauce over and mix some more. Chill. Carol recommends making this the morning of the potluck so that the flavors have a chance to mingle.

ZITI AND CAULIFLOWER

·

1 medium onion, chopped

3 cloves garlic, pressed

3 tablespoons olive oil

4 tablespoons butter

1 2-ounce can anchovies

1 small head cauliflower, broken
 into small flowerets

3 tablespoons tomato paste plus 2
 cups water

1 teaspoon dried basil

3 teaspoons capers

½ cup grated Cheddar cheese

1 pound ziti, cooked al dente and
 drained

Sauté the onion and garlic in the combined oil and butter. Add the anchovies and cook until they are broken up. Add the cauliflower and the tomato mixture; simmer for 4 minutes. Add the basil and capers and simmer for 15 minutes more.

Sprinkle the cheese over the ziti and cover with the sauce. Toss and serve.

CAVATELLI WITH BROCCOLI

·

from Joyce Struthers

NELSON, NEW HAMPSHIRE

1 head broccoli

2 tablespoons olive oil

8 ounces mushrooms, sliced

3 cloves garlic

¼ teaspoon salt

⅛ teaspoon pepper

1 pound cavatelli or other short
 pasta

6 tablespoons butter, melted

½ cup grated Parmesan cheese

*R*emove the broccoli flowerets from the stem and break into bite-sized pieces. Tender portions of the stem can also be used, pared, and cut into 1-inch pieces. Steam until just tender. Drain.

Heat the olive oil in a large skillet over medium heat. Add the mushrooms, broccoli, garlic, salt, and pepper, and sauté for about 4 minutes.

Cook the cavatelli according to package directions (probably about 12 to 15 minutes), drain thoroughly, but do not rinse.

Transfer the cavatelli to a serving bowl. Pour the melted butter over the cavatelli and toss. Add the broccoli mixture and the Parmesan cheese and toss until mixed.

THE GREAT SPAGHETTI
AND OLIVE CAPER

5 tablespoons olive oil
1 tablespoon minced fresh oregano
  or 1 teaspoon dried
1 tablespoon minced fresh basil or
  1 teaspoon dried
1 large clove garlic, pressed
One 16-ounce can peeled whole
  tomatoes

½ cup each stuffed green olives
  and black olives, sliced
2 tablespoons capers
1 cube chicken bouillon
1 pound spaghetti

*I*n a saucepan, bring the oil to medium heat and sauté the oregano, basil, and garlic for just a couple of minutes. Add the tomatoes, olives, capers, and bouillon and simmer for 30 minutes; stir occasionally.

When the spaghetti is al dente, drain and toss with sauce.

BAKED PASTA WITH LATE SUMMER VEGETABLE SAUCE

∎

TOPPING

1 clove garlic
3 tablespoons olive oil

1 cup fresh bread crumbs

¼ cup olive oil
1 cup chopped onion
1 cup cut-up green pepper
   (½-inch pieces)
2 cups cut-up young zucchini
   (½-inch lengths)
1 clove garlic, pressed
2 cups cut-up tomato (1-inch
   chunks)

1 tablespoon minced fresh basil or
   1 teaspoon dried
1 tablespoon minced fresh oregano
   or 1 teaspoon dried
Salt and pepper to taste
2 cups pasta (macaroni, rigatoni,
   shells, rotini, or similar pasta)

Sauté the garlic in the oil for 1 minute. Remove the garlic and discard. Stir in the bread crumbs and sauté for about 5 minutes or until the crumbs are golden. Set aside.

For the sauce, heat the oil in a large saucepan. Sauté the onion for a few minutes, until translucent. Stir in the green pepper, zucchini, and garlic and sauté for about 5 minutes. Add the tomato, basil, and oregano and simmer for about 20 minutes. Add salt and pepper.

While the sauce is simmering, cook the pasta. When the pasta is al dente, drain and combine with the sauce into a lightly oiled 2-quart baking dish. Top with the bread crumbs and bake in a preheated oven at 350°F for 20 minutes.

MACARONI MILANESE

•

from Gordon's Aunt Sally Spiegel

MADISON, CONNECTICUT

Sally has served this as a main dish for her Fourth of July gatherings for the last fifteen years.

¼ cup olive oil
2 cloves garlic, crushed
1 pound mushrooms, sliced
1 pound ground beef
One 12-ounce can tomato juice
One 34-ounce can Italian plum
  tomatoes, drained
One 2-ounce can flat anchovies,
  chopped
2 tablespoons chopped parsley

1 teaspoon dried basil
1 teaspoon dried oregano
6 to 7 drops Tabasco sauce
1 teaspoon salt
1 pound zucchini, sliced
1 pound macaroni shells, cooked
  and drained
1 pound cherry tomatoes,
  stemmed

Heat the oil in a 2½-quart skillet. Sauté the garlic and mushrooms until golden. Add the ground beef, breaking it up as it browns. Stir in the tomato juice, tomatoes, anchovies, parsley, basil, oregano, Tabasco, and salt. Cover and simmer over low heat for 1½ to 2 hours, stirring occasionally. Add the zucchini and cook 10 to 15 minutes more. Stir in the cooked macaroni and cook for 5 to 10 more minutes. Garnish with the cherry tomatoes and serve.

NOTE This recipe also works fine without the meat.

CURRIED SPAGHETTI

·

from Jan Dreschler

BELLE MEAD, NEW JERSEY

On tour with my contra dance band, I frequently stay in the homes of people who are dancers, musicians, and also avid potluck goers. Jan Dreschler is all three, and when we were staying at her house, I asked her if she had any good recipes or good stories about potlucks.

It turns out that for years she has made this curried spaghetti to bring to local supper gatherings. She has been approached, at times almost belligerently, to give out the recipe but has always refused for fear that if people knew how easy it was (they already knew how good it was), they'd all start bringing it and she'd have to make something else. Most persistent among her inquisitors was her otherwise dear friend Janet Peters. Finally, on the occasion of Janet's wedding, Jan presented her with the recipe, albeit with a restriction against bringing it to potlucks within a certain radius of the Princeton, New Jersey, area.

Later I happened to run into Jan and Janet (sitting next to their husbands, Bob Mills and Robert Mills, respectively) at a folk festival. Imagine Janet's indignation when she found out that Jan had let the recipe slip into my hands for eventual publication. I mumbled something about how Jan had also forced me to agree to a geographical restriction. We actually never discussed what the consequences might be. All I can say is that if you live in that part of New Jersey, you bring it to a potluck at your own risk.

—G.P.

1 medium onion, chopped
2 teaspoons curry powder
3 tablespoons butter
3½ cups chicken broth
8 ounces spaghetti

1 medium green pepper, diced
¼ cup diced red pepper
¼ cup sliced stuffed green olives
4 hard-boiled eggs, sliced
1 ripe tomato, sliced

$\mathcal{I}$n a 4-quart pan, sauté the onion and curry in the butter. When the onion is translucent, add the broth and bring to a boil. Add the spaghetti and keep on a gentle boil for 15 minutes. Stir in the green pepper, red pepper, and olives; cover and simmer for 5 minutes. Remove the cover and continue simmering if necessary to evaporate any additional liquid.

Serve out of the pot or transfer to another dish. Garnish with the eggs and tomato slices.

CRAB SPAGHETTI
GIOVANNI

—————

•

6 to 8 ounces fresh or frozen
  crabmeat
2 cloves garlic, minced
½ cup chopped onion
⅓ cup olive oil
½ cup pitted and chopped ripe
  olives
2 tablespoons chopped pimiento
¼ cup minced parsley

½ cup coarsely chopped walnuts
2 teaspoons lemon juice
½ teaspoon salt
⅛ teaspoon pepper
¼ teaspoon dried basil
¼ teaspoon dried oregano
8 ounces spaghetti, cooked and
  drained
¼ cup grated Parmesan cheese

$\mathcal{T}$haw (if necessary), drain, and slice the crabmeat. In a large skillet sauté the garlic and onion in the oil. Add the crabmeat, olives, pimiento, parsley, walnuts, lemon juice, and seasonings. Heat through. Toss the crab sauce with the hot spaghetti. Top with the Parmesan.

GORDON'S VEGETABLE
LASAGNA

■

12 lasagna noodles
½ pound mushrooms, sliced
1 small zucchini, cut into short
  strips
One 10-ounce package frozen
  chopped spinach, thawed and
  blotted dry
One 10-ounce package frozen
  chopped broccoli, thawed and
  blotted dry
1 pound ricotta cheese

3 eggs
½ teaspoon salt
¼ teaspoon pepper
3 cups Gordon's Tomato Sauce
  (see page 100)
1 pound mozzarella cheese,
  coarsely grated
1 cup finely grated Parmesan
  cheese
¼ cup chopped parsley

Cook the lasagna noodles according to package directions and store in cold water (they are much easier to handle when cool). Drain well for a couple of minutes before using.

Steam or sauté the mushrooms and zucchini lightly. Set aside. Thoroughly mix the spinach, broccoli, ricotta, eggs, salt, and pepper in a large bowl.

To assemble, spread ½ cup of the tomato sauce in the bottom of a 10-by-15-inch Pyrex glass or stainless steel baking dish. Set 4 noodles on the bottom (3 lengthwise and 1 across). Spoon in the spinach-ricotta filling and cover with another layer of noodles, reversing which end gets the crosswise piece. Spread the mushrooms and zucchini over the second noodle layer, and cover with the mozzarella and 1 cup of the tomato sauce. Add the final layer of noodles. Sprinkle on the Parmesan and parsley, and cover with the remaining sauce.

Bake, uncovered, in a preheated oven at 350°F for 45 minutes and let cool for 30 minutes before serving, or bake for 35 minutes and reheat later.

NOTE Since the sauce listed here is seasoned, there is no need for additional seasoning. If you are using another sauce and wish to add more seasonings, mix them in with the spinach-ricotta mixture.

GREEN AND WHITE
LASAGNA

•

Our friend Steve Zakon provided us with this recipe for a tomatoless lasagna.

1 pound lasagna noodles
Two 10-ounce packages frozen
 chopped spinach, thawed
2 pounds cottage cheese
3 eggs, beaten
1 pound mozzarella cheese, grated

4 ounces Parmesan cheese, grated
3 to 4 cloves garlic, pressed
1 tablespoon dried basil
¼ teaspoon pepper
2 teaspoons milk
A few shakes of paprika

Cook the lasagna noodles according to package directions and store in cold water (they are much easier to handle when cool). Drain well for a couple of minutes before using.

Mix the spinach and cottage cheese together and then add the eggs, three quarters of the mozzarella, the Parmesan, garlic, basil, and pepper. Mix well.

Pour the milk into a 9-by-13-inch baking dish—just enough to cover the bottom. Put in one layer of noodles and spread over with a third of the cheese-spinach mixture. Set in another layer of noodles, perpendicular to the first layer, and another third of the mixture. Repeat this process once more, using up the cheese mixture. Top with a final layer of noodles and spread over with the remaining mozzarella cheese. Sprinkle with paprika.

Bake, covered, in a preheated oven at 375°F for 45 minutes and then uncovered for 10 minutes more. Let stand 15 minutes before cutting.

NOTE This is actually better if made the day before and reheated. If you're doing it this way, bake the first day for 35 minutes, covered. Store in the refrigerator. Then reheat for 30 minutes, covered.

TOFU LASAGNA

■

from Alice Freeman

NEWFANE, VERMONT

¼ cup butter
12 ounces mushrooms, thinly
  sliced
5 cloves garlic, finely chopped
1 teaspoon salt
¼ teaspoon pepper
1 quart tomato sauce (see
  page 100 for Gordon's
  recipe)

1 cup wheat germ
2 cups mashed tofu
½ cup grated Parmesan cheese
1 cup grated mozzarella cheese
½ cup chopped parsley

Melt the butter in a large skillet. Add the mushrooms, garlic, salt, and pepper and cook until the mushrooms are tender, about 5 minutes. Stir in the tomato sauce, reserving just enough to line the baking dish, and the wheat germ. Heat thoroughly.

Combine the tofu and Parmesan in a small bowl. Combine the mozzarella and parsley in another bowl.

Spread a thin layer of sauce in the bottom of a 9-by-13-inch baking dish. Set down one third of the noodles and spread half of the tofu mixture on top. Pour one third of the sauce mixture over the tofu and top with one third of the mozzarella. Repeat layering, then make the final layers of noodles, sauce, and mozzarella.

Bake uncovered in a preheated oven at 350°F for 45 minutes. Let stand for 15 minutes before cutting. Garnish with chopped fresh parsley.

SPINACH-STUFFED MANICOTTI

·

from Celeste Hewson

THOMPSON STATION, TENNESSEE

1 package manicotti (14 shells)
1 pint cottage cheese
One 10-ounce package frozen
 chopped spinach, thawed and
 drained
1 egg

1 cup grated mozzarella cheese
1 teaspoon chopped parsley
½ teaspoon dried basil
2 cups tomato sauce (your
 favorite)
¼ cup grated Parmesan cheese

Cook the manicotti as directed. When cooked, rinse the manicotti and hold in cold water to cool and to keep the shells from closing in and sticking to themselves.

Mix everything except the tomato sauce and grated cheese and fill the manicotti shells. Set them in a 9-by-13-inch pan and cover with the tomato sauce. Top with the Parmesan and bake in a preheated oven at 350°F for 35 minutes.

SESAME NOODLES

•

The versatility of foods is often discovered by accident, which is no doubt how cooking has evolved over the centuries. We once had a potluck in our home and were proudly preparing both this recipe and the Spicy Beef and Plum Sauce (page 142). In the confusion of getting everything out on the table, I inadvertently poured this peanut sauce over the beef (which was intended to have plum sauce). Being among understanding friends, I promptly confessed my mistake. We all agreed that the plum sauce on the noodles probably wouldn't be very good, but the beef (which we then tossed with the soba noodles) turned out quite tasty. Here, however, we have written the recipe as it was intended to be. Feel free to experiment.

We originally obtained the sauce recipe from Polly Bannister of Greenfield, New Hampshire, who learned how to make it from Becky Nordstrom of Amherst, Massachusetts.

—G.P.

SAUCE

2 tablespoons peanut butter
5 tablespoons soy sauce
2 tablespoons freshly grated ginger
2 cloves garlic, minced

½ cup brown or white rice-wine
  vinegar
¾ cup sesame oil
3 drops hot oil

1 pound buckwheat soba noodles

¼ cup slivered scallions

ℳix all the sauce ingredients in a blender. Cook the noodles according to package directions, then pour the sauce over and sprinkle with the scallions.

NOTE The noodles will cook in less than 5 minutes, so it is good to prepare the sauce ahead of time. The sauce will keep for other things and can also be frozen.

NOODLES WITH CHICKEN
AND PEANUT SAUCE

■

8 ounces spaghetti or other thin
  noodles
4 teaspoons cornstarch
1½ cups water
2 tablespoons peanut butter
2 tablespoons soy sauce
2 tablespoons cider vinegar
2 tablespoons sugar

2 teaspoons ground coriander
2 tablespoons grated fresh ginger
6 scallions, slivered
1 tablespoon vegetable oil
12 ounces boneless, skinless
  chicken, cut into bite-sized
  chunks
4 cups bean sprouts

Cook the pasta according to package directions. To make sauce, dissolve the cornstarch in 2 tablespoons of the water, then add the peanut butter and stir until smooth. Add the remaining water and the soy sauce, vinegar, sugar, coriander, ginger, and two thirds of the scallions. Heat the oil in a wok or heavy skillet. Stir-fry the chicken over high heat for 5 minutes. Remove with a slotted spoon and set aside. Reheat the remaining oil and stir-fry the bean sprouts for 2 minutes. Return the chicken to the pan, add the sauce, and heat for 1 minute more, stirring, until the sauce thickens. Toss with the drained pasta, and garnish with the remaining scallions.

Six

VEGETABLE

DISHES

■

RATATOUILLE

•

One of my favorite things to find at a potluck is Ratatouille, that savory blend of eggplant, zucchini, tomatoes, and other vegetables. I have concluded that many others share my taste, for the "rat" dish always seems to be one of the first to be emptied. If I have to forgo some items on the table the first time through the line, I make sure that at least I've got as large a helping of Ratatouille as decent manners permit. I pass that advice on to my fellow "rat" enthusiasts.

One solution to the problem is to bring the Ratatouille yourself. This doesn't necessarily mean you'll get more at the potluck, but you can sample it beforehand, and you can save aside a little bit for a delicious omelet the next morning.

—G. P.

½ cup olive oil
4 cloves garlic, thinly sliced
1 large onion, quartered and
   quartered again
1 medium eggplant, cut into
   ½-inch cubes
2 young zucchini, sliced into
   ¾-inch pieces
1 green pepper, cut into 1-inch
   squares (seeds reserved)
1 yellow or red pepper, cut into
   1-inch squares (seeds reserved)

½ teaspoon dried thyme
1 tablespoon dried basil
1 tablespoon dried oregano
½ teaspoon pepper
4 ripe tomatoes, quartered and
   quartered again, or one
   28-ounce can peeled whole
   tomatoes
Salt to taste
½ cup grated Parmesan cheese

In a large skillet, heat 2 tablespoons of the olive oil and sauté the garlic and onion until the onion is translucent. Remove with a slotted spoon into a large bowl.

Add ¼ cup more oil and sauté the eggplant and zucchini until they are tender. Remove into the bowl with the onion.

Add the remaining oil and sauté the peppers, thyme, basil, oregano, and black pepper. (Note: You can toss the pepper seeds right in with this too.) When the peppers are tender, add the tomatoes and cook for about 5 minutes, until the tomatoes have lost some of their liquid. Again using a slotted spoon, remove this mixture into the bowl. Mix everything together and taste to determine the need for salt.

Sprinkle on the Parmesan and mix in lightly. Turn everything into a casserole dish and bake uncovered in a preheated oven at 350°F for 30 minutes.

CURRIED BAKED CAULIFLOWER

■

Our neighbor Denise Kearns brought this down to our house one night for supper. She got the recipe from her mother-in-law, Daphne Witsell.

1 large head cauliflower	1 teaspoon curry powder
½ teaspoon salt	¼ cup bread crumbs or crushed
1 cup grated Cheddar cheese	croutons
⅓ cup mayonnaise	2 tablespoons melted butter
⅔ cup plain yogurt	

*B*reak the cauliflower into flowerets and steam for 10 minutes. Meanwhile, in a large bowl, stir together the salt, cheese, mayonnaise, yogurt, and curry powder. Add the cauliflower and mix well. Pour into a 2-quart casserole. Toss the bread crumbs in the melted butter, sprinkle onto the cauliflower, and bake uncovered in a preheated oven at 350°F for 30 minutes or until it is hot and bubbly.

BROCCOLI-AND-CHEDDAR
CASEROLE

·

This and the Blue Broccoli below could be made with frozen broccoli, but they will be superior with fresh.

2 pounds (or more) broccoli
3 eggs, beaten
3 cups cottage cheese
¾ cup grated Cheddar cheese

½ cup minced scallions
2 tablespoons butter
½ cup wheat germ
¼ cup grated Parmesan cheese

℃hop the broccoli and steam until just tender. Set the broccoli in a 9-by-13-inch baking dish or similar-sized casserole. Combine the eggs, cheese, and scallions and pour over the broccoli.

Melt the butter and stir in the wheat germ. Cook for just a minute or two.

Sprinkle the Parmesan over the broccoli. Top with the wheat germ. Bake in a preheated oven at 350°F for 25 minutes.

BLUE BROCCOLI

·

2 pounds broccoli
2 tablespoons butter
2 tablespoons flour
3 ounces cream cheeese, softened

¼ cup crumbled blue cheese
1 cup milk
½ cup Ritz cracker crumbs (about 10 crackers)

℃hop the broccoli and steam until just tender. In a large saucepan, melt the butter and blend in the flour and both cheeses. Add the milk, stirring constantly, until it comes to a boil. Stir in the broccoli. Place in a 1-quart casserole and top with the cracker crumbs. Bake in a preheated oven at 350°F for 30 minutes.

MOM'S SWEET POTATO CASSEROLE

·

from Julie Rohr

NELSON, NEW HAMPSHIRE

Julie and her husband, Walter, joined us for a Thanksgiving feast a couple of years ago. One of the highlights of the meal was the casserole that Julie brought.

TOPPING

½ cup light-brown sugar	1 cup chopped walnuts or pecans
⅓ cup flour	½ cup melted butter

3 cups mashed cooked sweet potatoes	1 teaspoon vanilla
	½ cup butter, melted
2 eggs, beaten	1 teaspoon ground cinnamon

Combine the brown sugar, flour, and nuts and stir into the melted butter. This will be quite thick. Combine the sweet potatoes and the remaining ingredients and spread in a roundish casserole dish. Spread the topping over the sweet potato mixture. Bake uncovered in a preheated oven at 350°F for about 40 minutes, until the topping is golden and a bit crispy. Reheat at destination.

SWEET POTATO PIE

———
•

For a variation on the theme, try:

¼ cup light-brown sugar
2 tablespoons maple syrup
4 tablespoons melted butter
½ cup milk
1 egg
¼ teaspoon salt

⅓ teaspoon ground cinnamon
3 dashes ground nutmeg
2 cups grated raw sweet potato
  (peeled before grating)
Juice and grated rind of 1 orange

Mix together the sugar, syrup, butter, milk, egg, salt, cinnamon, and nutmeg. Stir in the sweet potato, orange juice, and rind. Pour into an 8-inch square baking dish or 9-inch pie plate. Bake in a preheated oven at 325°F for 1 hour.

Good hot or cold.

CARROT CASSEROLE

•

from Julie Rohr

NELSON, NEW HAMPSHIRE
———

1½ pounds carrots (4 cups cut
  up)
½ cup bread crumbs
¼ cup grated Parmesan cheese

1 teaspoon onion salt
1 cup diced green pepper
4 tablespoons melted butter
1 cup grated Cheddar cheese

$\mathcal{P}$eel and cut the carrots into sticks about 3 inches long and ½ inch thick. Cook until tender, drain, and reserve the water. Set half the carrots in a casserole dish.

Mix the bread crumbs, Parmesan, and onion salt. Spread half of this over the carrots, and then spread half of the peppers on top.

Repeat the layering process. Pour over 2 tablespoons of the carrot water and the melted butter. Top with the Cheddar cheese. Bake uncovered in a preheated oven at 400°F for 15 minutes.

SUMMER SQUASH CASSEROLE

■

from Mary Bevilacqua

WELLESLEY, MASSACHUSETTS

2 medium or 3 small yellow
  summer squash
2 medium or 3 small zucchini
8 ounces sour cream
½ cup chicken broth

2 carrots, peeled and shredded
2 cups poultry stuffing or bread
  crumbs
¾ cup butter, melted

$\mathcal{C}$ut the squash and zucchini into bite-sized pieces. Blanch, drain, and cool. In a large bowl, combine the sour cream, chicken broth, and carrots. Then mix in the squash and zucchini.

In another bowl, mix the stuffing or bread crumbs with the melted butter. With half of the stuffing, line the bottom of a 9-by-13-inch pan. Pour in the squash mixture and then top with the remaining stuffing. Bake, uncovered, in a preheated oven at 350°F for 30 minutes.

CORN PUDDING

·

from Celeste Hewson

THOMPSON STATION, TENNESSEE

4 cups canned corn, drained
 (frozen or fresh corn may also be
 used, but should be cooked
 slightly and drained)
1 teaspoon sugar

3 tablespoons butter, melted
4 eggs, slightly beaten
4 cups scalded milk
1 teaspoon savory

Mix the corn, sugar, butter, eggs, and milk and put into a 3-quart buttered baking dish. Sprinkle with the savory. Bake uncovered in a preheated oven at 350°F for 45 minutes.

POTATO PIE

·

This recipe calls for baked potatoes, so cook some extra ahead of time or use up leftovers.

5 large potatoes, baked
1 cup cottage cheese
1 cup ricotta cheese
⅓ cup milk or cream
2 tablespoons butter
3 eggs
1 cup grated Parmesan cheese

2 tablespoons minced onion
2 tablespoons chopped chives
2 tablespoons chopped parsley
¼ teaspoon salt
¼ teaspoon pepper
¼ cup bread crumbs

Scoop out the potatoes from their skins. (You won't use the skins for this recipe, but you can put them to good use elsewhere.) Mix the potatoes with the cottage cheese, ricotta, milk or cream, and butter. Beat in the eggs and add ¾ cup of the Parmesan. Add the onion, chives, parsley, salt, and pepper.

Thoroughly butter a large low casserole dish and sprinkle a mix of the bread crumbs and remaining Parmesan over it, so that it is completely coated. Shake to evenly distribute any remaining loose crumbs. Pour the potato mixture into this and bake uncovered in a preheated oven at 350°F for 35 to 45 minutes, until puffy and brown.

MASHED POTATO
CASSEROLE

.

from Carolyn Edwards

FITZWILLIAM, NEW HAMPSHIRE

This makes a good use of leftover mashed potatoes.

*2 cups mashed potatoes (hot or
cold)
One 8-ounce package cream
cheese, softened
1 small onion, finely chopped*

*2 eggs, at room temperature
2 tablespoons flour
Salt and pepper to taste
Seasoned bread crumbs*

Put the potatoes in a large mixer bowl. Add everything except the bread crumbs and beat at medium speed until light and fluffy.

Spoon into a greased 9-inch baking dish, sprinkle with the bread crumbs, and bake, uncovered, in a preheated oven at 300°F for 35 minutes.

This should be reheated on location. This recipe is very easy to modify, according to the quantity of mashed potatoes you have.

BACON-AND-POTATO PIE

.

1 pound Canadian bacon

8 eggs

½ pound sharp Cheddar cheese,
 coarsely grated

1 medium onion, chopped

½ teaspoon pepper

3 to 4 potatoes, peeled

Cut the Canadian bacon into thin slices and then into 1-inch squares. Fry in a skillet until browned. Drain and blot on paper towels to degrease.

Beat the eggs until foamy. Mix in the cheese, onion, pepper, and bacon.

Coarsely grate the potatoes into a bowl of cold water. Transfer to a colander and drain well, pressing the potatoes with a large spoon to remove extra moisture.

Combine the potatoes with the egg-bacon-cheese mixture, and pour into a greased 9-by-13-inch baking dish. Bake uncovered in a preheated oven at 350°F for 45 minutes. Let set for a few minutes before cutting into squares of desired size.

DILLY BEANS

.

from Rich Hart and Wendy Rannenberg

AMHERST, NEW HAMPSHIRE

This recipe was the very first contribution we received for this book. Rich and Wendy are such potluck enthusiasts that they plan months in advance. The original recipe that they submitted began with the sowing of cayenne pepper seeds in March. More horticultural instructions followed, including details of planting the beans, dill, and garlic. Although space limitations deter us from including everything, we will pass on the tip that they recommend "Provider" beans from Johnny's Selected Seeds.

Next followed instructions for harvest, sometime in August. Finally, the final part of the recipe, which we include below. We first enjoyed these Dilly Beans when Rich and Wendy joined us for Thanksgiving one year. Since then, we find them occasionally at potlucks when Rich doesn't have time to make his excellent bread.

By the way, Rich and Wendy got married in Nelson a couple of years after we did. Inspired by our wedding, they too had a potluck reception.

EQUIPMENT

Six 1½-pint wide-mouthed canning jars
Canning kettle

Nonreactive enameled pan for boiling vinegar solution

3¼ cups white vinegar
3¼ cups water
6 tablespoons un-iodized salt
3 pounds straight string beans, fresh off the vine

3 cayenne peppers
6 heads dill
6 to 12 cloves garlic

*P*lace the jars in the canning kettle and bring to a boil. In a small pan, sterilize the canning lids. In the enameled pan, bring the vinegar, water, and salt to a boil.

Wash the beans and trim the ends. Cut the length, if necessary, so that the beans will fit into the jars. Remove the sterilized jars one at a time from the canning kettle. Into each jar, place as many beans as will fit (pack them in well), half a cayenne pepper, 1 head of dill, 1 large or 2 small garlic cloves, and the vinegar solution, to ¼ inch from the top.

Cover tightly and return to the kettle for a boiling water bath for 10 minutes. Remove from kettle and let cool naturally. When cool, store the beans for a few weeks before using. The day before the potluck, chill the Dilly Beans in the refrigerator.

CREAMY TOMATO ASPIC

∎

from Mary Sheldon

PETERBOROUGH, NEW HAMPSHIRE

---

2 envelopes unflavored gelatin
½ cup cold water
One 16-ounce can tomatoes
1 teaspoon chopped onion

½ teaspoon salt
½ teaspoon celery salt
1 teaspoon sugar
2 tablespoons vinegar
½ cup sour cream

Soften the gelatin in the cold water. In a saucepan, heat all the ingredients except the sour cream to boiling. Add the gelatin mix and stir until dissolved. Rub the mixture through a sieve or blend in a food processor. Blend in the sour cream.

Cool slightly, then pour into a greased 3-cup mold, rinsed in cold water. Chill for 3 hours. Unmold and serve with mayonnaise.

Seven

MEAT, POULTRY,

AND SEAFOOD

■

It is not unusual at potluck suppers to be standing while you eat or perhaps trying to balance a thin paper plate on your knee while you go at your dinner. With this in mind, we have designed or revised all of our meat recipes so they can be eaten without the use of a knife.

While some of the recipes in this section can be served cold or at room temperature, it is important to remember that meat (especially chicken) will spoil if it is held at room temperature for a long time. If you are traveling a long distance, or if you are arriving well ahead of the eating hour, be sure to refrigerate these or any other meat dishes, and then reheat if necessary.

CHICKEN

Buying boned chicken will save you time but not money. Most of our chicken recipes begin with the meat already skinned and off the bone. If you are going to do this step yourself, be sure to allow extra time for that. In most cases, chicken legs can be left bone in, since the bone serves as a handle. We do not specifically call for using legs in any of these recipes, but if you prefer dark meat, there's no reason not to use them.

HUNGARIAN CHICKEN
PAPRIKA

■

2 cups flat noodles	2 teaspoons dried thyme
2 whole chicken breasts, skinned and boned	1½ cups flour
1 cup lemon juice	2 tablespoons paprika
3 medium onions	Salt and pepper to taste
½ cup olive oil	12 ounces mushrooms
2 tablespoons butter	1 pint sour cream
	1 cup chicken broth

The noodles may be cooked according to package directions any-time in advance. If they are ready well ahead of time, store them in cold water to keep from drying out. Drain well before using.

Cut the chicken into small chunks (about the size of your thumb, but please don't get them confused) and set in a bowl and soak in the lemon juice.

Slice the onions (either lengthwise or crosswise) and sauté in a skillet with ¼ cup of the olive oil and the thyme. When the onions become translucent, transfer to the casserole dish you will be using.

Mix the flour, paprika, and salt and pepper. Roll the chicken pieces in this mixture to coat them, and brown lightly in the skillet with the remaining olive oil. Remove to the casserole dish.

Melt the butter in the skillet and sauté the mushrooms lightly. Add to the casserole dish. Stir in the cooked noodles, sour cream, and chicken broth. Cover and bake in a preheated oven at 350°F for 30 minutes.

CHICKEN CARUSO

•

Merle Peery is an excellent and innovative cook. When she and Russell decided to leave New England and resettle in Tennessee, we lost the opportunity for several wonderful meals over the course of the year. This is one of the recipes she sent us.

8 ounces elbow macaroni or pasta of your choice	2 cups cubed cooked chicken or turkey
4 cups chicken broth	One 10-ounce package frozen green peas
3 slices bacon	2 cups coarsely grated sharp Cheddar cheese
½ cup finely chopped green pepper	¼ cup toasted slivered almonds
½ cup finely chopped red pepper	3 tablespoons sherry
⅓ cup finely chopped onion	

Cook the macaroni in the chicken broth according to the cooking time on the box. *Do not drain!* In a large, heavy skillet, fry the bacon until crisp. Remove to paper towels to absorb the grease. Add the peppers and onion to the skillet and cook until tender. Drain off the bacon fat. Combine the macaroni and broth with the remaining ingredients, and mix thoroughly. Everything is ready at this point and can be placed in a casserole to be heated when needed. Bake covered in a preheated oven at 350°F for 30 to 45 minutes.

POPEYED CHICKEN WITH
PEANUT SAUCE

·

We enjoy experimenting with different applications for the peanut sauce recipe on page 113. This is one of our more recent discoveries.

2 chicken breasts, skinned, boned, and cubed
4 cloves garlic
½ teaspoon chili powder
½ teaspoon ground oregano
½ teaspoon dried thyme
½ teaspoon ground rosemary
½ teaspoon ground cumin
½ teaspoon celery seed

½ teaspoon ground coriander
1 tablespoon sesame oil
Two 10-ounce boxes frozen spinach
One 8-ounce package buckwheat soba noodles
1½ cups peanut sauce (see page 113)

Lightly cook the chicken cubes, garlic, and herbs in the oil. The spinach may be used as is if thawed in time, otherwise cook just enough to thaw. Cook the noodles in boiling water for 3 minutes or until tender. Drain. In a greased 2-quart casserole dish, set in one third of the noodles, a layer of half of the spinach, a layer of half of the chicken, and a layer of the second third of the noodles. Pour half the peanut sauce evenly over the noodles. Repeat the layering process and cover with the remaining peanut sauce. Cover and bake in a preheated oven at 350°F for 30 minutes.

CHICKEN SALAD WITH FRUIT AND RICE

■

This is a tasty summer dish with a lot of variety in every bite. Since the chicken meat is cooked before it is cut, it can also be made with leftover chicken.

3 whole chicken breasts (or
  equivalent leftovers)
1¼ cups chicken stock (from
  cooking) or broth
2 tablespoons butter
¾ cup rice (uncooked)
2 tablespoons dry vermouth
Grated rind of 1 lemon
¼ cup chopped parsley

1 cup seedless grapes
One 16-ounce can pineapple
  chunks, drained
1 cup pine nuts or slivered
  almonds
1 cup chopped celery
¾ cup mayonnaise
Salt and pepper to taste
½ cup sliced pitted ripe olives

Cook the chicken breasts by placing in boiling water and reducing to a simmer for 20 minutes or until the chicken is done. Remove the breasts and cool. Reserve 1¼ cups of the stock. If you are using leftover chicken, you will need to provide other stock or broth.) When the chicken is cool, remove the skin and bones and cut the meat into bite-sized pieces.

In a saucepan, melt the butter and add the rice, stirring for about 2 minutes. Add the vermouth and stock or broth and bring to a boil. Reduce the heat, cover, and simmer for 25 minutes or until the liquid has been absorbed. Let the rice cool, then mix with the chicken, lemon rind, parsley, grapes, pineapple, pine nuts or almonds, and celery. Mix in the mayonnaise. Season with salt and pepper. Garnish with the ripe olives.

MEXICAN CHICKEN SALAD

·

Rich and spicy.

2 large or 3 small chicken breasts, skinned and boned	2 teaspoon chili powder
	1 teaspoon ground cumin
2 tablespoons butter	2 cups sour cream
3 cloves garlic, pressed	½ cup chopped tomato
¾ cup water	½ cup chopped scallions
1 tablespoon or 3 cubes chicken bouillon	½ cup chopped green pepper

Cut the chicken breasts into thin strips and sauté in the butter with the garlic. When the chicken is just browned, add the water, bouillon, chili, and cumin. Cover and simmer for 8 minutes or until the chicken is tender and cooked. Stir in the sour cream and heat through. Spoon into the serving dish.

Garnish the top with the tomato, scallions, green pepper, and any other vegetable of your choice. This is especially nice served on a bed of lettuce with either taco shells or chips on the side. Don't set it out on the tacos, as they will get soggy. This is good warm but fine cold too.

TURKEY LOAF

■

This loaf is best served cold, so prepare it in advance.

1 large onion, diced
2 tablespoons butter
½ teaspoon paprika
¼ teaspoon dried thyme
2 eggs
½ cup plain yogurt
3 slices of bread, crumbled, or 1
  cup fresh bread crumbs

½ cup chopped parsley
1 teaspoon salt (or to taste)
¼ teaspoon pepper
1½ pounds ground turkey
¾ cup pimiento-stuffed green
  olives

Sauté the onion in the butter with the paprika and thyme. Beat the eggs lightly, mix with the yogurt, and mush the bread into it. Combine the onion-herb mixture, egg-yogurt mixture, parsley, salt, pepper, turkey, and olives. Set into a greased bread pan and bake in a preheated oven at 400°F for 1 hour or until the loaf is firm. Let cool, wrap tightly in foil, and refrigerate. Slice just before serving. (It's easier at the potluck to have it already sliced.)

MEATLOAF

·

There's meatloaf, and then there's Meatloaf. We believe we've mastered the secret to the latter with this recipe.

1 cup milk

2 cups stale bread, crackers, or
 croutons (or some of each)

2 pounds ground beef

½ cup peanut butter (optional)

1 cup finely diced carrots

1 medium onion, diced

3 cloves garlic, pressed

½ cup chopped parsley

1 teaspoon salt (or to taste)

½ teaspoon pepper

2 teaspoons chili powder

One 6-ounce can tomato paste

2 teaspoons Worcestershire sauce

Splash of red wine

6 to 10 mushrooms

Pour the milk into a large mixing bowl and mix the bread, crackers, or croutons into it so that the milk gets absorbed. After that has happened, take all the remaining ingredients except the mushrooms and put them in the bowl. Roll up your sleeves, wash your hands, and get right into it. After all the ingredients are more or less uniformly distributed, form into one long loaf (in a 9-by-13-inch baking dish) or two shorter ones (you can use bread pans). Clean the mushrooms, trim the ends, and press them all the way, tail first, into the top of the meatloaf over its entire length.

Bake in a preheated oven at 350°F for 1½ hours. Drain off the liquid from the pan before serving or taking to the potluck. If the loaf is to be served warm, it might be best to let each person slice his or her own. Cold meatloaf is perfectly acceptable to serve (some folks like it better). It is easier to slice and can be sliced ahead, allowing for more efficient serving.

SHERRIED MEATBALLS

from Alice Freeman

NEWFANE, VERMONT

Alice says, "This dish wowed 'em at potluck church suppers in Williamstown, Massachusetts, during the '50s and is still getting compliments in the '90s."

4 slices bacon	1 pound ground beef
1 medium onion, minced	1 egg
1 clove garlic, minced	¼ teaspoon pepper
¼ cup fine bread crumbs	¼ teaspoon dried oregano
3 ounces dried mushrooms	½ cup dry sherry or apple cider
2 tablespoons butter	

Cook the bacon until crisp, then drain on absorbent paper. Pour off most of the fat from the pan. Sauté the onion and garlic in the remaining fat over low heat for 5 minutes; add the crumbs and cook a few minutes longer. Separately, sauté the mushrooms in the butter, just enough to cook off the liquid. Mix together everything except the bacon, and form into 12 to 15 balls.

Crumble the bacon into little bits. Roll each meatball in the bacon bits. Set the meatballs in a baking dish, cover, and bake in a preheated oven at 375°F for 45 minutes.

SWEET AND SOUR
MEATBALLS

•

This makes about four dozen meatballs. The quantity can be easily varied to suit your needs.

1½ *pounds ground beef*
1 *cup fresh bread crumbs*
 (2 *slices*)
1 *egg*
1 *tablespoon beef bouillon*

1 *tablespoon chopped parsley*
2 *tablespoons lemon juice*
1 *cup apricot preserves*
1 *tablespoon sweet relish*

Make 1-inch or slightly larger meatballs using the beef, bread crumbs, egg, and 2 teaspoons of the bouillon. Brown in a large skillet. Remove with a slotted spoon and pour off the fat. In the skillet, combine the remaining bouillon, parsley, lemon juice, apricot preserves, and sweet relish. Cook, stirring regularly, over low heat for 15 minutes. Add the meatballs, cover, and simmer for 10 minutes.

MACARONI-HAMBURGER CASEROLE

MACARONI-HAMBURGER CASSEROLE

•

from Merle Peery

COLUMBIA, TENNESSEE

Merle has found this recipe to be a big hit with kids (as well as grown-ups).

3 cups macaroni
4 tablespoons vegetable oil
1 large onion, diced
1 green pepper, diced
1 or 2 cloves garlic, mashed
1 pound ground beef
One 16-ounce can tomatoes
2 tablespoons tomato paste
  [an unlikely amount to have
  on hand]

1 teaspoon paprika
½ teaspoon dried oregano
½ teaspoon dried basil
1 tablespoon chopped fresh
  parsley or ½ tablespoon dried
1 teaspoon Worcestershire sauce
2 teaspoons Angostura bitters
  (optional)
1 cup coarsely grated sharp
  Cheddar cheese

The macaroni may be cooked ahead or started while everything else is being done. Cook according to package directions. Heat the oil in a large, heavy skillet and sauté the onion, green pepper, and garlic. As soon as they are limp, add the beef and stir frequently until browned. Add the tomatoes, tomato paste, paprika, herbs, and seasonings. Mix with the cooked macaroni and half of the cheese, and pour into a 2-quart casserole or 9-inch square baking dish. Top with the remaining cheese. Cover and bake in a preheated oven at 375°F for 30 minutes; uncover and bake for an additional 10 to 15 minutes.

NOTE If covering with foil, grease the underside of the foil first so it won't stick to the cheese.

SICILIAN SUPPER

———
∎

When I was growing up in Middletown, Connecticut, I always looked forward to the short drive down to Madison, on the shore of Long Island Sound, to visit my paternal grandparents. Certain memories remain quite vivid: going to the beach, helping my grandfather in the garden, and playing with assorted friends and cousins. Best of all, we had great meals.

We still drive down to Madison, though now it is from New Hampshire, so the trips aren't as frequent. Our children walk on the beach and "work" in the garden with their great-grandparents. Best of all, we still have great meals there.

My grandmother, Nancy Peery, sent us this recipe.

—G.P.

2 cups noodles
1½ pounds ground beef
½ cup chopped onion
One 6-ounce can tomato paste
¾ cup water
1 teaspoon salt
¼ teaspoon pepper

¾ cup milk
One 8-ounce package cream
  cheese
1 clove garlic, minced
1 cup chopped green pepper
½ cup grated Parmesan cheese

Cook the noodles in advance according to package directions. Brown the meat and add the onion. Sauté until lightly cooked. Add the tomato paste, water, salt, and pepper. In a separate pan, heat the milk, then add the cream cheese and stir until smooth. Stir in the garlic, green pepper, noodles, and half of the Parmesan. Add more milk if this mixture seems too thick.

In a casserole dish, make alternate layers of the meat and noodles, starting and ending with the meat. Sprinkle the remaining Parmesan over the top and bake, uncovered in a preheated oven at 350°F for about 25 minutes or until heated through.

LOUISE'S HAMBURGER CASSEROLE

—————
•

Nancy Peery also sent us this recipe. The name derives from the fact that she got the recipe from Cousin Louise in California.

1 pound ground beef
1 cup chopped celery
1 medium onion, diced
½ cup rice (uncooked)
½ cup water

½ tablespoon soy sauce
½ cup sour cream
½ cup chicken broth
1 cup slivered almonds
2 cups chow mein noodles

Sauté the meat, onion, and celery. Stir this into a 2- or 3-quart (preferably flat and shallow rather than deep) casserole dish with the rice, water, soy sauce, sour cream, and chicken broth. Cover and bake in a preheated oven at 300°F for 1½ hours. Spread the nuts and noodles on top for the last 15 minutes of baking time.

SHEPHERD'S PIE

▪

from Alice Freeman

NEWFANE, VERMONT

Alice calls this "Hamburger Pie." She notes: "This was a great childhood favorite of mine and my brother's and sister's. We used to gravitate to it at church suppers because of our certainty of its provenance. My children, however, think it's repulsive because it mixes foods together."

It is very similar to a Shepherd's Pie that Gordon's mother used to make, so we've decided to call it that. We've actually come across lots of recipes for Shepherd's Pie, and the determining ingredient seems to be the mashed potato topping. This is a good way to use up leftover mashed potatoes (if there is such a thing), and you should feel free to vary the recipe to use anything else that's cluttering up the refrigerator or hanging out in the garden.

1 medium onion
2 tablespoons butter
1 pound hamburger
1 tablespoon Worcestershire sauce
3 cups frozen or fresh chopped
  vegetables

One 10¾-ounce tomato soup
  (undiluted)
2 cups (or more) mashed potatoes
Paprika to taste

Sauté the onion in 1 tablespoon of butter, add the hamburger, and cook lightly. Cook the vegetables as necessary. Add the vegetables, tomato soup, and Worcestershire sauce to the meat and mix together. Put this all in a greased casserole dish and cover with the mashed potatoes. Sprinkle remaining melted butter over the potatoes, and also some paprika. Bake uncovered in a preheated oven at 350°F for 30 minutes.

SAVORY STEAK

·

Mary Sheldon, a colleague of Susan's, has lived and traveled all over the world with her husband, Wes, who was in the diplomatic corps. She has collected many things, including this recipe. She notes: "This was given to me by a friend from New Zealand thirty years ago!"

1 pound chops or braising steak, sliced
Vegetable oil
½ cup chopped onion
½ cup chopped celery
½ cup hot water
2 teaspoons curry powder
3 tablespoons ketchup

2 tablespoons Worcestershire sauce
2 tablespoons vinegar
2 tablespoons brown sugar
2 teaspoons beef-flavored concentrate (such as Bovril or Marmite)
A few dashes of Tabasco sauce

Sear the meat in a small amount of oil and put in a casserole. Cover with the chopped onion and celery. Drain off the fat from the skillet, loosen the brown bits left from the meat, and add the ½ cup hot water to make a gravy. Add the remaining ingredients and stir until hot. Pour over the meat. Cover and bake in a preheated oven at 325°F for 1 hour.

This is good served with rice or noodles.

SPICY BEEF AND PLUM
SAUCE

∎

This is one of our favorites. On the remote chance that there are any leftovers, you can make yummy pocket sandwiches with it the next day.

2 pounds boneless beef sirloin
  steak
3 tablespoons sesame oil
2 tablespoons dry sherry
½ cup tamari

2 tablespoons cornstarch
2 tablespoons brown sugar
2 teaspoons crushed red pepper
1 cup chopped scallions

PLUM SAUCE
1 cup vegetable oil
¾ cup plum sauce (available in
  Oriental section of supermarket)

¾ cup red wine vinegar
2 cloves garlic, pressed
½ cup sugar

Lettuce and tomato for garnish

Cut the beef into ⅛-inch strips (this is easier if it is partially frozen). Mix 1 tablespoon of the oil with the sherry, tamari, cornstarch, brown sugar, and red pepper. Pour this over the steak and refrigerate for 30 minutes or more.

In a wok or large skillet, sauté the scallions quickly over high heat in 1 tablespoon of the oil. Leave the heat high and stir-fry the meat (half at a time—remember to add another tablespoon of the oil with the second half of meat). The meat and scallions can be set aside in a large bowl.

Blend the plum sauce ingredients together and pour over the beef. Set the entire mixture on a platter or in a serving bowl, garnished with lettuce and tomato.

BEEF AND PASTA SALAD

■

This is a good recipe for making the day before a potluck.

1 pound rotini pasta
1 pound boneless beef sirloin steak

2 tablespoons vegetable oil
1 teaspoon Worcestershire sauce

DRESSING
3 cloves garlic, pressed
½ teaspoon salt
¼ cup lemon juice or balsamic
  vinegar (you can also use
  flavored vinegars such as chive,
  garlic, or dill)

1 teaspoon Dijon mustard
½ teaspoon freshly ground black
  pepper
1 teaspoon ground oregano
1 teaspoon ground basil
¾ cup olive oil

6 ounces provolone cheese, cubed
½ cup pitted ripe olives
8 to 10 cherry tomatoes, halved

½ pepper (green, red, or yellow)
1 cup artichokes (cut into smaller
  pieces)

Cook the pasta so that it will be done about the same time the beef is done.

Cut the beef into thin strips. Heat the oil in a skillet and brown the beef. Add the Worcestershire sauce and stir before setting aside. Drain the pasta, mix with the beef, and set aside.

Mash the garlic into the salt to make a paste. Then beat in the lemon juice or vinegar and let set for however long it takes for you to do something else. Add the mustard, pepper, oregano, and basil, and mix well. Add the oil and blend or shake before pouring over the pasta-beef mixture.

Chill for a while. Shortly before serving, mix in any of the remaining ingredients.

JACKIE DIEHL'S
HAM DAINTIES

■

Mary Sheldon got this recipe from a neighbor in Virginia.

BUTTER SPREAD

1 pound butter, at room temperature

6 tablespoons poppy seeds

6 tablespoons prepared mustard

6 dozen finger rolls (homemade or store-bought)

1 medium to large onion, finely chopped

2 teaspoons Worcestershire sauce

1½ pounds boiled ham, shredded

⅔ pound Swiss cheese, shredded

*B*lend the spread ingredients together. Split the dinner rolls. Spread the tops and bottoms with the butter spread, and add layers of ham and cheese. Wrap individually in foil and bake at 400°F for 10 minutes, or set on a cookie sheet and cover the entire lot with foil, then bake.

Wrap surplus dainties individually in foil and freeze for use another time. Frozen dainties should be baked for 15 minutes.

HAM AND NOODLE CASSEROLE

·

You know how it is when you get a craving for a baked ham. You buy it, bake it, serve it up with mashed potatoes and carrots. A week goes by and you've been living on ham and eggs for breakfast and ham sandwiches for lunch, and it still takes up as much room in the refrigerator as it did when you it put it in there. You can't bear to throw it away, but you know that if you're going to eat another bite of it, it's got to be made into something really different.

2 cups noodles	½ cup milk
2 cups diced ham	2 teaspoons Dijon mustard
¼ pound mushrooms, sliced	1 cup sour cream
¼ cup minced onion	½ cup bread crumbs
1 cup chopped cauliflower (or one 10-ounce package frozen)	1½ tablespoons butter, melted
1 tablespoon vegetable oil	½ cup grated cheese (Cheddar or Swiss or combination)
8 ounces chicken broth	

Cook the noodles as indicated on the package. Drain and combine with the ham. In a large skillet, sauté the mushrooms, onion, and cauliflower in the oil. When the vegetables are just tender, stir in the broth, milk, mustard, and sour cream.

In a greased casserole dish, layer half the noodle-ham mixture and then half the vegetable-sauce mixture. Repeat. Toss the bread crumbs with the melted butter and sprinkle over the casserole. Top with the grated cheese. Bake, uncovered, in a preheated oven at 350°F for about 30 minutes.

PORK AND RICE
CASSEROLE

·

This recipe comes from Nancy Peery, Gordon's grandmother. She makes it with whole pork chops, which is a great way to do it if it's not going to be used for a potluck.

1 pound pork sirloin cutlets
2 tablespoons vegetable oil
¼ teaspoon salt
½ teaspoon pepper
1 cup white rice (uncooked)

¼ teaspoon dried thyme
½ cup diced onion
½ cup diced green pepper
2½ cups chicken broth

Cut the meat into small cubes and brown in the oil in a skillet or a heavy iron baking pot. Add the salt and pepper and remove from the pan. Loosen any meat bits and add the rice and thyme to the drippings. Cook, stirring, for 2 or 3 minutes or until the rice starts to brown. Add the onion and green pepper. Transfer to a casserole dish if necessary (or bake in the baking pot). Pour in the chicken bouillon and set the pork on top. Bake, uncovered, in a preheated oven at 350°F for 45 minutes or until the liquid is absorbed.

LAMB SALAD

·

MARINADE
1 small onion
2 cloves garlic
½ teaspoon ground cumin
1 tablespoon lime juice

2 teaspoons grated fresh ginger
2 tablespoons soy sauce
1 tablespoon sugar

1 pound boneless ½-inch-thick
   lamb steaks

DRESSING
2 tablespoons peanut butter
2 tablespoons lime juice
1 teaspoon soy sauce
1 teaspoon brown sugar

¼ teaspoon salt (or to taste)
½ teaspoon grated fresh ginger
¼ teaspoon cayenne pepper
2 tablespoons peanut oil

1 pound green beans
1 large pepper (yellow, orange, or
   red)

Peanuts and fresh cilantro for
   garnish

Blend the marinade ingredients until smooth. Pour over the lamb in a glass dish just large enough to hold it. Let set for several hours or overnight.

In a bowl, mix together the dressing ingredients, holding out the oil until all the other ingredients are mixed thoroughly.

Grill or broil the lamb to medium rare. Let cool and then cut into julienne strips. Trim and boil the beans in water until just tender. Drain, rinse in cold water, drain again, and set aside. Seed and cut the pepper into julienne strips.

Mix the lamb, beans, and pepper together in a large bowl and add the dressing. When it is thoroughly dressed, set it in a serving dish and garnish with peanuts and fresh cilantro.

CUMIN MEATBALLS

·

1 pound lean ground lamb
1 egg, slightly beaten
½ cup bread crumbs
¼ cup milk
2 tablespoons minced onion

1 tablespoon minced parsley
1 teaspoon ground cumin
½ teaspoon salt
¼ teaspoon pepper
2 tablespoons vegetable oil

Wash your hands. Put everything except the oil in a bowl and mix together until combined. Make meatballs ½ inch in diameter. Wash your hands again.

Heat the oil in a large skillet and cook the meatballs, shaking the pan to turn them regularly. They should cook in about 5 minutes. Remove with a slotted spoon or spatula and set on a serving plate, or set on a cookie sheet or in a baking pan to be reheated just prior to serving (about 15 minutes in a preheated oven at 325°F).

SALMON-BROCCOLI
CASSEROLE

·

One 10-ounce package frozen
  chopped broccoli
⅓ cup chopped onion
½ cup diced celery
¼ pound mushrooms, sliced
1 tablespoon butter
One 7¾-ounce can salmon

1 cup sour cream
¼ cup grated Parmesan cheese
½ teaspoon dried dill
½ teaspoon salt
⅛ teaspoon pepper
2 tablespoons lemon juice

haw the broccoli in advance. Sauté the onion, celery, and mush-rooms in the butter until tender.

Drain the salmon and reserve the liquid. Stir the liquid into the onion and add the sour cream. Heat through. Add the Parmesan, dill, salt, pepper, and lemon juice. Toss with the broccoli and salmon, transfer to a buttered baking dish, and bake covered in a preheated oven at 350°F for 20 minutes.

SALMON KEDGEREE

·

One 15½-ounce can red salmon
2 cups water
1 teaspoon salt
1 cup rice (uncooked)
¾ cup chopped onion
2 cloves garlic, minced

¼ cup butter
¼ teaspoon salt
½ teaspoon curry powder
⅛ teaspoon crushed red pepper
2 hard-boiled eggs, sliced
2 tablespoons chopped parsley

Drain and flake the salmon. Bring the water to a boil. Add the 1 teaspoon salt and the rice. Bring to a boil and reduce the heat. Cover and simmer 20 to 25 minutes.

In a large skillet or pot, sauté the onion and garlic in the butter. Add the salmon, the rice, the ¼ teaspoon salt, the curry, and the red pepper. Heat through.

Serve from the pot or place in a serving dish. Garnish with the eggs and parsley.

Eight

SAVORY PIES

■

WORKING WITH PHYLLO PASTRY

We buy our phyllo in a frozen package of twenty-six sheets labeled fillo, which, along with filo, is apparently an accepted American-ized spelling. In Greek it is spelled ΦΥΛΛΟ and it means "leaf." Our recipes were devel-oped for nine-by-thirteen-inch sheets of phyllo (designed to conform to standard cook-ware). We've seen phyllo in larger sheets, which are a little more difficult to handle. The exact number of layers to use is quite flexible, so don't worry about folding over or overlap-ping sheets if you need to modify the recipe to a different size sheet.

Anyone who has worked with this paper-thin Greek pastry has probably experienced an initial period of frustration as it stuck to itself or to the work surface, or as it became brittle and broke apart when you were trying to assemble it. Neophylloites should heed these remarks—the stuff can be tricky. But don't get scared off. There are some basic techniques that will increase the likelihood of success.

The biggest problems with phyllo come from insufficient thawing before use and drying out during use. Take the frozen package from the freezer and put it into the refrigerator overnight, or at least for a few hours. Then set the unopened package out at room temperature for an hour or two. Don't force the thaw—that will just make it sticky. If you must hurry, remove the plastic package from the cardboard box, but don't set it in a warm location. You can tell when it is ready by how flexible the roll feels: It will be limp when you pick it up.

Before you open the package, prepare the filling and melt the butter. Have a small paint brush or pastry brush (one that's not too stiff) ready. Brush the pan with butter and then open the package. From this point on, procedure varies with the recipe, but in all cases it is important to work as quickly as possible, without interruption, to finish before the phyllo dries out. Although the package instructions say that the phyllo can be refrozen if it is tightly rewrapped, our recommendation is to plan to use the entire package at once. With the flat pan recipes such as Spanakopita (opposite) this is no problem. If you're making tiropita, you may not want to make so many of one thing. Two suggestions: Either cut the filling recipes in half and do two different kinds of triangles, or assemble them all and freeze half of them (unbaked and well wrapped).

Reheating: When a phyllo dish is stored in the refrigerator, the dough tends to become a little moist and soggy. This is best remedied by reheating it in a regular oven (or even a toaster oven) rather than a microwave oven.

SPANAKOPITA

•

It was this Greek spinach pie that first brought phyllo pastry to my attention many years ago. I have experimented with many variations of the filling, only to come back to the basic spinach and feta cheese. It can also be prepared in roll fashion (see Cheese and Mushroom Roll, page 155) or in little triangles, with the same quantity of filling (use about 1½ tablespoons per triangle).

—G.P.

Two 10-ounce packages frozen
　chopped spinach, thawed and
　squeezed dry
1 pound feta cheese
½ teaspoon pepper

3 eggs
1 tablespoon dried oregano
½ cup butter, melted
One 8-ounce package phyllo
　pastry, thawed (see page 151)

Mix all the ingredients except the butter and phyllo together in a big bowl. The feta may need to be crumbled by hand. Brush a 9-by-13-by-2-inch cake pan with the butter. Open the phyllo and lay 5 sheets in the pan, buttering each one. Spread the spinach mixture evenly over the top. Layer the remaining phyllo, buttering each sheet as before. Tuck the edges down into the pan with a kitchen knife or spatula. With a sharper knife, make slits through the top phyllo layers to let moisture out.

Bake in a preheated oven at 350°F for 45 minutes or until the top begins to brown. Allow to set for a few minutes before cutting into whatever size squares you want.

MEAT, SPINACH, AND CHEESE PIE

———— ■ ⌐ ————

This version introduces some new tastes—meat, tomato, mint—to Spanakopita (page 153).

MEAT FILLING
1½ cups chopped onion
2 tablespoons olive oil
1½ pounds ground beef or lamb
¾ teaspoon salt
¾ teaspoon pepper

1 teaspoon dried oregano
⅓ cup tomato paste
¾ cup grated Parmesan cheese
2 eggs, beaten

SPINACH AND CHEESE FILLING
½ cup chopped scallions
1 tablespoon olive oil
Two 10-ounce packages frozen
  spinach, thawed and drained
¾ cup chopped parsley
¼ cup chopped fresh dill or
  1 tablespoon dried

¼ cup chopped fresh mint or
  1 tablespoon dried
1 teaspoon pepper
3 eggs, beaten
½ pound feta cheese
½ pound ricotta cheese

One 8-ounce package phyllo
  pastry, thawed (see page 151)

½ cup butter, melted

For the meat filling, sauté the onion in the oil until tender. Add the meat and cook until browned. Drain off the excess fat and combine the meat mixture with the remaining meat filling ingredients.

For the spinach and cheese filling, sauté the scallions in the oil, and when they are tender, add the spinach and cook for no more than 5 minutes. Mix with the remaining filling ingredients.

Follow the guidelines in the Spanakopita recipe (page 153) for working with and buttering the phyllo, using the same size 9-by-13-by-2-inch pan. When the bottom layers have been prepared, add the meat filling and then the cheese filling. Cover with the remaining phyllo, again as described on page 153. Bake in a preheated oven at 350°F for 45 minutes.

CHEESE AND
MUSHROOM ROLL
•

This makes one large flaky roll, which is easy to transport. If you take it to a potluck, reheat briefly before slicing.

½ cup butter
¼ pound mushrooms, sliced
½ cup sour cream
2 cups grated cheddar cheese

2 teaspoons dried oregano
One 8-ounce package phyllo
 pastry, thawed (see page 151)

In 1 tablespoon of the butter, sauté the mushrooms lightly, stir in the sour cream, and set aside. Melt the remaining butter in a small saucepan over low heat. When the butter is melted, brush cookie pan, open the phyllo, and stack in layers on a cookie pan, buttering each sheet separately with a light pastry brush or paint brush. After 3 or 4 sheets have built up, sprinkle on a layer of cheese and just a pinch or two of oregano and continue. When about half of the phyllo is used (there should be 2 or 3 layers of cheese at this point), add the mushrooms, spreading evenly over the surface. Then continue layering the phyllo and adding more layers of cheese until the phyllo is all used up. Put in any remaining cheese and oregano at this point.

Using a scraper or metal spatula, lift a long side of the rectangle and roll it up like a rug. Butter the outside generously and poke a few holes with a sharp knife so that it can breathe. Bake in a preheated oven at 350°F for 45 minutes. Cut into 1-inch slices.

CHEESE PIE

•

Susan Lord gave us this delicious recipe. The components can be prepared a day ahead and the pie baked the day you want to eat it. The pie travels well, and it's tasty at any temperature. It can be gently reheated at 300°F for fifteen minutes.

Susan and David Lord were part of a "Potluck Community Choir," a group of friends that gathered for food and song. They'd sit around and cook up stuff like:

> *This food is your food, that food is my food.*
> *From Cauliflornia to the New York icebergs,*
> *From the red-leaf cabbage to the Gulf Stream watercress,*
> *This food is made for you and me.*

CRUST

1½ cups unbleached flour (or use ¾ cup unbleached and ¾ cup whole wheat)
Pinch of salt

1 tablespoon sugar
½ cup butter
1 to 2 tablespoons ice water

FILLING

2 large eggs
¾ cup light cream
1 pound cheese, at least 2 varieties (e.g., 8 ounces Swiss and 8 ounces Cheddar)
4 tablespoons flour
4 tablespoons butter (more if needed)

1 large onion, sliced
10 ounces spinach, chopped
8 ounces mushrooms, sliced
3 cloves garlic, minced
2 large ripe tomatoes, sliced
1 tablespoon chopped fresh basil
Freshly grated nutmeg

For the crust, combine flour, salt, and sugar. Cut in the butter with a pastry blender to form coarse particles. Toss with the ice water until the dough coheres. Roll out the dough and line a deep-dish pie pan (one that holds at least 4 cups of liquid).

For the filling, beat the eggs with the cream and set aside. Grate the cheeses separately and toss each in a bowl with 2 tablespoons flour. Remove the cheese and spread it in the pie shell, discarding any excess flour. In a heavy frying pan, melt the butter and sauté separately, in turn, the onion, spinach, mushrooms, and garlic, and finally the tomatoes with the basil. Use more butter if necessary. As each vegetable becomes tender, remove with a slotted spoon, leaving the butter in the pan. Layer the vegetables on top of the cheese. Top the tomato layer with the other cheese, again discarding excess flour.

All of these steps can be done a day ahead if you like. Whenever you are ready to bake the pie, pour the egg and cream mixture over the pie, being careful not to overflow the edge of the crust. Grate the nutmeg over the top. Bake in a preheated oven at 350°F for 45 minutes to 1 hour or until the top just starts to brown. Let cool 15 minutes or so before serving.

CORN AND PIMIENTO PIE

■

2 cloves garlic
½ cup butter, melted
1 pound corn (frozen or canned)
2 eggs
1 pound Cheddar cheese, grated

Salt and pepper to taste
1 small jar whole pimientos
One 8-ounce package phyllo
   pastry, thawed (see page 151)

Crush the garlic into the melting butter. If canned corn is used, drain it well. Frozen corn can be used as is. Mix with the eggs and cheese, and add salt and pepper to your liking. Cut the pimientos into thin strips. Brush a 9-by-13-by-2-inch cake pan with the garlic butter. Open the phyllo and lay 5 sheets in the pan, buttering each one after it is set in. Add the corn filling and spread out evenly, then set the pimiento strips across the top. Layer the remaining phyllo, buttering each sheet as before. Tuck the edges down into the pan with a kitchen knife or spatula. With a sharper knife, make slits through the top phyllo layers to let moisture out.

Bake in a preheated oven at 350°F for 45 minutes or until the top begins to brown. Allow a few minutes to set before cutting into whatever size squares you want.

PHYLLO PIZZA

■

This makes a rectangular pizza—cut small squares to make great-looking appetizers. This recipe makes two pizzas. Additional toppings of your choice can be added: peppers, mushrooms (sauté first), onions, olives, and of course they can be varied between the two pans.

2 cloves garlic
½ cup butter, melted
½ cup finely grated Parmesan
  cheese
¾ cup grated mozzarella cheese

1 tablespoon dried basil
1 tablespoon dried oregano
4 or 5 ripe tomatoes, thinly sliced
One 8-ounce package phyllo
  pastry, thawed (see page 151)

Crush the garlic into the melting butter. Brush some of the garlic butter onto 2 cookie sheets. Open the phyllo and start layering, buttering between each layer and sprinkling just a pinch or two of the Parmesan and just a few flakes of the basil and oregano between each layer. After half the phyllo is used, start the other cookie sheet in the same way. Top with the tomatoes and any other toppings of your choice. Use up any remaining Parmesan and herbs on the top and then cover with the mozzarella.

Bake in a preheated oven at 350°F for 30 minutes or until sides are crisp.

TOFU-BROCCOLI QUICHE

·

Our neighbor and friend Denise Kearns gave us this recipe. The wheat germ crust is a nice fast alternative to preparing pastry. Like the Cheese Pie (page 156), this tastes good at any temperature.

WHEAT GERM CRUST
¾ cup wheat germ
3 tablespoons margarine, melted

3 tablespoons grated Parmesan
cheese

FILLING
1 head broccoli, broken into
flowerets
3 eggs
½ teaspoon salt
¼ teaspoon ground nutmeg

⅛ teaspoon pepper
1 pound soft tofu, well drained
1 medium onion, minced
½ cup grated Cheddar cheese

Mix all the crust ingredients in a bowl. Put in the center of a pie plate and spread evenly toward the edges and up the sides, pressing down firmly. Bake for 8 minutes in a preheated oven at 350°F before filling.

Steam the broccoli until crisp-tender. Put the eggs, salt, nutmeg, and pepper in a food processor or blender and mix. While the appliance is on, add the tofu a quarter pound at a time. Blend until smooth. Combine the egg-tofu mixture, broccoli, onion, and cheese. Pour into the partially baked wheat germ crust. Bake at 350°F for 30 to 40 minutes or until the filling is set. Serve warm or at room temperature. Refrigerate for longer storage.

RUSSIAN VEGETABLE PIE

·

The Vegetarian Epicure by Anna Thomas inspired many of us to try this sturdy pie, which can be served hot or cold. This is Gordon's latest version.

PASTRY FOR DOUBLE-CRUST PIE

2 cups flour
½ teaspoon salt

4 ounces cream cheese
½ cup butter or Crisco

FILLING

1 small head purple cabbage
½ teaspoon caraway seed
2 tablespoons butter
3 carrots, thinly sliced
½ pound mushrooms, sliced
1 medium onion, sliced
1 clove garlic, minced
Salt and pepper to taste
⅛ teaspoon ground rosemary
¼ teaspoon dried thyme

4 ounces cream cheese, at room
  temperature
1 apple, peeled and cut into thin
  slices
4 hard-boiled eggs, peeled and
  sliced
Several sprigs dill, chopped
Egg wash (1 egg beaten with
  1 teaspoon water)

For the crust, mix flour and salt. Cut in the cream cheese and the butter or Crisco, adding a tablespoon of cold water if necessary to make a dough that coheres. Chill the dough while you make the filling.

Chop the cabbage and sauté it with the caraway seed in the butter. Add the carrots, mushrooms, onion, and garlic and sauté, stirring all the while, until the vegetables are soft. Add the salt, pepper, rosemary, and thyme. Divide the pie pastry in half and roll out one half to line a 9-inch pie plate. Spread the cream cheese in the bottom of the pie shell. Add a layer of apple slices, a layer of sliced eggs, and the cooked vegetables. Sprinkle with the dill. Roll out the top crust and place over the pie, crimping the edges to seal. Cut steam vents in the top of the pie. Paint with the egg wash. Bake in a preheated oven at 425°F for 15 minutes, then reduce the heat to

350°F and bake an additional 25 minutes, until the crust is starting to brown. Serve hot or cold. (The pie, or individual portions, may be frozen or reheated.)

TAMALE PIE

•

1 pound ground beef (or use half
  ground beef and half bulk Italian
  sweet sausage)
½ cup chopped onion
3 garlic cloves, minced
1 cup tomato sauce (canned or
  homemade)
½ cup pitted and sliced ripe olives
2 to 3 teaspoons chili powder (or
  to taste)

1 teaspoon ground cumin
2½ cups water
¾ cup yellow cornmeal
½ teaspoon salt
2 tablespoons butter
1 cup shredded Cheddar or
  Monterey Jack cheese
½ cup broken corn chips or taco
  chips

In a heavy skillet, brown the meat and break it up. Remove the browned meat to a bowl and pour off most of the fat. Sauté the onion and garlic in the skillet until soft, then stir in the tomato sauce, olives, chili powder, and cumin. Simmer for a few minutes and set aside. Bring the water to a boil in a medium saucepan. Add the cornmeal and salt and cook, stirring constantly, until the mixture is thick (about 10 minutes). Stir in the butter. Spread the cornmeal mixture into a greased 8-by-8-inch or 10-by-6-inch baking dish. Spoon the meat mixture over the cornmeal. Sprinkle with the cheese and chips. Bake in a preheated oven at 350°F for about 30 minutes, until hot and bubbly. Let stand for at least 5 minutes before serving so the pie firms up.

SALMON QUICHE WITH CHEDDAR-ALMOND CRUST

·

If you're feeling ambitious, make a double recipe and freeze one quiche after baking (wrap well; to use, thaw and bake, covered, for about twenty minutes in a preheated oven at 350°F).

CRUST

1 cup whole wheat flour
2/3 cup grated Cheddar cheese
1/2 cup chopped almonds

1/2 teaspoon salt
1/4 teaspoon paprika
4 tablespoons butter, melted

SALMON FILLING

One 15½-ounce can red salmon, drained and with any bones removed
3 eggs, well beaten
1 cup sour cream

½ cup grated Cheddar cheese
¼ cup mayonnaise
1 tablespoon grated onion
1 teaspoon chopped fresh dill
Dash of Tabasco sauce

For the crust, mix the flour, cheese, almonds, salt, and paprika in a medium bowl. Add the melted butter and stir to blend. Reserve ½ cup for the topping. Pat the rest firmly onto the bottom and sides of a 10-inch quiche pan or pie plate. Bake in a preheated oven at 400°F for 10 minutes while you mix the filling. Remove the pie shell from the oven and reduce the heat to 325°F.

Place the salmon in a bowl and break up with a fork. Combine with the rest of the filling ingredients and pour into the partially baked pie shell. Sprinkle with the reserved crumbs. Bake at 325°F for about 45 minutes, until the center is firm. Cool for 5 minutes before serving. This is also good at room temperature.

TOMATO AND ASPARAGUS
QUICHE

■

One 10-inch pie shell, baked for
  10 minutes at 400°F
4 eggs, beaten
3 tablespoons flour
½ teaspoon paprika
½ teaspoon salt
1 teaspoon dry mustard

1½ cups half-and-half
2 cups grated cheese, 1 cup Swiss
  and 1 cup Cheddar
10 fresh asparagus spears
1 ripe tomato, cut into 6 thin
  slices

While the pie shell bakes, beat the eggs with the flour, paprika, salt, dry mustard, and half-and-half. Stir in the cheese. Wash and trim the asparagus spears. Saving the 6 most perfect ones for the top, cut the other 4 into bite-sized pieces. Lay the chopped asparagus on the partially baked pie shell and pour the cheese mixture over the top. Bake at 350°F for about 20 minutes. Remove from the oven and quickly arrange the 6 tomato slices and the 6 asparagus spears on the quiche, with the asparagus forming "spokes" of a wheel and the tomato rounds in between. Return to the oven and bake 20 minutes longer, until the quiche is firm. Let cool for 5 to 10 minutes before serving. Tastes good at room temperature too.

Nine

YEAST BREADS, QUICK BREADS, MUFFINS, AND MORE

■

BREADS

Occasionally, and usually over a meal, we get into a "favorite foods" discussion with friends. What's your favorite vegetable? (I usually vacillate between carrots and potatoes.) If you became a vegetarian, what meat would be hardest to give up? For me, it would be beef, if only for the charcoal-grilled hamburgers on crusty hard rolls found exclusively in my hometown, Sheboygan, Wisconsin, burger Mecca.) Or, what food could you eat every day and never get sick of?

Now, that's easy. There already *is* one food I eat every day and never get tired of: bread. I've been baking bread for more than twenty years now and have never tired of the process or the product.

Bread baking has an undeserved reputation for being time-consuming and difficult. Actually, you can work it into your life quite easily, and the dough, when handled in a reasonable way, is virtually indestructible. Yeast really *wants* to rise and grow, just like a seed in the garden. You can slow it down (in the refrigerator) or speed it up, if you must, by putting the bread bowl on a heating pad set on low heat (I discourage this, however, as it can too easily result in dry, overrisen bread). You can vary ingredients, substituting milk or buttermilk for water, molasses for sugar, throwing in some grated orange rind or raisins, stirring in a cup of oats or a scoop of millet. Once you get a feel for bread, you can improvise.

I remember the first loaf of yeast bread I ever tried: It was called Granny's Health Bread (this was the year of Woodstock, remember) and included nearly every grain known to mankind except regular old white flour. It didn't seem to rise much, but I baked it anyway. Whole civilizations could be built from little bricks like the ones I made.

My bread baking has evolved somewhat, fortunately. Most of the time today I use a cool-rise, sponge method when baking bread (see Basic Everyday Bread, pages 168–69). I let the sponge bubble overnight, and sometime the next morning I complete the dough and put it in the refrigerator to rise. This system offers great flexibility, and I can work in the bread making around weekend household chores or family activities. Also, the long rising makes the bread more flavorful.

Most of the yeast bread recipes that follow call for less yeast than one might expect. In my experience, most recipes that call for two packages (two scant tablespoons) of dry yeast (usually to leaven about six cups of flour) will do just as well using just one package (one scant tablespoon). This small economy might slow down the rising somewhat, but it helps create a finer, tighter texture in the baked product. Because we live in New England, I'm able to use King Arthur flour (a high-quality unbleached, all-purpose flour) for all of my baking. If you can't obtain it, another brand of unbleached flour should give good results.

Bread is always welcome at a potluck, and if you have an extra loaf in your freezer, your contribution will be easy. If possible, bring a cutting board, knife, and stick of butter. In my opinion, the baker is always entitled to the heel, but you may have to have quick hands to get your due.

I have a heavy-duty mixer with a bread hook, which works fine, but after some experimentation I have found I prefer to knead by hand. Besides, I have two enthusiastic young helpers willing to punch their fists into the warm bread dough. Maybe that's why the bread tastes so good.

—S. P.

NEW YEAR'S DAY BREAD

·

Staying home and baking bread on New Year's Day is one way to start off the new year right. This is what I came up with on the first day of 1984 and have often made since then. It's a tender bread and makes good toast.

—S. P.

2 cups milk

¼ cup butter

¼ cup honey

2 teaspoons salt

1 package (1 scant tablespoon)
 dry yeast

½ cup warm water

1 cup wheat germ

1 cup rolled oats

2 cups whole wheat flour

3 to 4 cups unbleached flour

Scald the milk in a medium saucepan, remove from the heat, and let the butter melt in the hot milk. Add the honey and salt and set aside to cool to room temperature. In a large bowl, dissolve the yeast in the warm water. Add the milk mixture, wheat germ, oats, and whole wheat flour. Beat until smooth. Add the unbleached flour a cup at a time until you have a dough that leaves the sides of the bowl. Turn the dough onto a floured board and knead until the dough is smooth and elastic (it will bounce back when you poke it). Wash the bowl in hot water, dry well, and grease the inside. Place the ball of dough in the bowl, turn over so the greased side is up, and cover the bowl with a wet towel or plastic wrap. Let the dough rise until doubled, about 1 hour. Punch down, divide in half, and shape into 2 loaves. Place in greased bread pans, cover lightly, and let rise until nearly doubled. Bake in a preheated oven at 400° F for about 30 minutes or until the loaves are golden and sound hollow when tapped. Turn out onto wire racks to cool. Makes 2 loaves.

Note Instead of loaves, you could shape the dough into 2 dozen rolls. Baking time will be slightly less.

BASIC EVERYDAY BREAD

·

I make bread nearly every weekend. I usually mix the sponge on Friday night and finish the bread sometime Saturday. The buttermilk contributes tenderness; the wheat berries and millet, a fresh nutty taste and a certain bite.

—S. P.

SPONGE

1 package (1 scant tablespoon)
  dry yeast

2 cups warm water
2 cups unbleached flour

1 cup buttermilk
2 teaspoons salt
¼ cup molasses or honey or
  brown sugar
⅓ cup vegetable oil (we use
  canola)

1 cup wheat berries (available in
  health food stores)
1 cup millet (available in health
  food stores)
1 cup rolled oats

6 to 7 cups unbleached flour
   (amount depends on humidity of
   air and flour) or enough to make
   a smooth dough

Egg wash (1 egg beaten with
   1 teaspoon water)

At least 12 hours before completing the dough, make the sponge: Sprinkle the yeast over the warm water in a large ceramic bowl and when the yeast is dissolved, stir in the flour to make a batter. Don't worry about a few little lumps. Cover the bowl securely with plastic wrap and let stand on the counter at room temperature for 12 to 24 hours.

When you are ready to complete the dough, warm the buttermilk to about 100°F (body temperature) in a medium saucepan (it may separate, but that's okay), and stir in the salt, molasses or alternative, and oil. Add to the sponge and stir well. Grind the wheat berries and millet in a grain mill (preferably), blender, or even in batches in a clean coffee mill. Stir the ground wheat and millet into the batter. Add the oats and 2 cups of the unbleached flour and beat well by hand or with a dough hook. Gradually add the remaining flour until the dough is kneadable (the dough should be soft, but will leave the side of the bowl). Do not add more flour than necessary. Turn onto a floured board and knead until the dough is smooth and elastic (it will bounce back when you poke it). Wash the bowl in hot water, dry, and grease the inside. Place the ball of dough in the bowl, turn over so the greased side is up, and cover with plastic wrap or a wet towel. The dough will rise and double at room temperature in about 1 to 1½ hours, or in the refrigerator in 2 to 3 hours. (Do whatever fits your schedule.) When the dough has doubled, punch down and shape into 3 loaves. Flatten each portion into a rectangle, roll up, pinch seam to seal, tuck ends under, and place seam-side down in greased bread pans. Cover lightly and let rise again until nearly doubled. Brush the tops with the egg wash. Bake in a preheated oven at 400°F for about 30 minutes, until the loaves are golden and sound hollow when tapped. Turn out onto wire racks to cool. Makes 3 good-sized loaves.

NOTE If you don't have a way to grind the wheat berries and millet, or if you can't obtain them, you can substitute 1 cup of wheat germ and an extra cup of rolled oats and get good results.

R Y E - W H E A T - Y O G U R T
B R A I D

·

2 cups rye flour
2 cups whole wheat flour
2 teaspoons salt
1 tablespoon caraway seed
(optional)
1 package (1 scant tablespoon)
dry yeast

1 cup milk
½ cup water
1 cup plain yogurt
½ cup molasses
¼ cup butter or margarine
3 to 3½ cups unbleached flour

Combine the rye and whole wheat flours with a whisk. In a large bowl, whisk together the salt, caraway seed if desired, yeast, and 1½ cups of the rye-wheat mixture. Heat the milk, water, yogurt, molasses, and butter or margarine just until the shortening melts (about 120°F, no hotter). Beat into the dry ingredients using an electric mixer or wooden spoon. Add 1 cup of the rye-wheat mixture and beat until smooth. Stir in the rest of the rye-wheat mixture and enough unbleached flour to make a soft dough. Turn onto a floured board and knead until smooth and elastic (the dough will bounce back when you poke it). Place in a greased bowl and turn to grease the top. Cover and let rise until doubled, about 1 hour. Punch down and divide into 6 equal pieces. Roll each piece into a rope about 18 inches long. Form into 2 braids, tuck the ends under, and transfer carefully to greased baking sheets (1 braid per sheet). Cover and let rise until nearly doubled, about 1 hour. Bake in a preheated oven at 375°F for 25 to 30 minutes, until the braids sound hollow when tapped. Remove from the baking sheets and cool on wire racks. Makes 2 braids.

CARDAMOM BREAD

This is a fine-textured bread that looks and tastes a little fancy. It make two good-sized loaves, or, if you are feeling festive, you can braid it into one large wreath (make sure it will fit onto a baking sheet!).

1 package (1 scant tablespoon)
  dry yeast
½ cup warm water
1 cup milk
½ cup butter
½ cup sugar
2 teaspoons ground cardamom
1 teaspoon salt

2 eggs, beaten
1 tablespoon grated orange peel
⅓ cup fresh orange juice
5 to 6 cups unbleached flour
1 cup golden raisins (optional)
Egg wash (1 egg yolk beaten with
  1 tablespoon cream)
1 tablespoon sugar

Sprinkle the yeast over the warm water in a large bowl. While it dissolves, heat the milk and butter in a large saucepan just until the butter melts. Remove from the heat. To this mixture add the sugar, cardamom, salt, eggs, orange peel, and orange juice and stir well. Stir the milk mixture into the yeast. A cup at a time, add the flour, beating well. Add the raisins if desired. When a very soft dough has formed, turn out onto a well-floured board and knead lightly. Place the dough in a clean, greased bowl and turn so the greased side is up. Cover with a damp towel and let rise until doubled, about 1 hour. Punch down and divide into 6 equal parts. Roll each part into a 16-inch rope. Make 2 loose braids, tuck the ends under, and place on greased baking sheets. (You could also bake the braids in greased bread pans.) Cover lightly and let rise again until nearly doubled. Brush each braid with the egg wash, sprinkle with the tablespoon of sugar, and bake in a preheated oven at 350°F for about 30 minutes (longer if you bake 1 large braid) or until the loaves sound hollow when tapped. If the braids brown too fast cover loosely with foil. Cool on wire racks. Makes 2 loaves.

MIKE'S HEALTH BREAD

•

Mike Patenaude of Mount Horeb, Wisconsin, was a "house hus-band" for a few years back when that was news. This bread, which he made regularly, supports life in a most satisfying way.

1 package (1 scant tablespoon)
  dry yeast
½ cup warm water
1 cup rolled oats
2 teaspoons salt
2 tablespoons butter or other
  shortening

1 cup raisins
2¾ cups boiling water
1 cup wheat bran or oat bran
¾ cup molasses
1 cup whole wheat flour
6 to 7 cups unbleached flour

Soften the yeast in the warm water in a small bowl. In a large bowl, combine the oats, salt, butter or other shortening, raisins, boiling water, and bran. Stir until the shortening melts and the mixture has cooled to about 110°F (no need to use a thermometer —just stick your finger in and see if it's pleasantly warm). Add the molasses, whole wheat flour, and enough unbleached flour to make a soft, kneadable dough. Turn out onto a floured board and knead firmly until smooth. The dough will bounce back when you poke it. Place in a greased bowl, turn the dough so the greased side is up, cover, and let rise until doubled, about 1 hour. Punch down and form into 2 large or 3 medium loaves, then place in greased bread pans. Cover and let rise again until nearly doubled. Bake in a pre-heated oven at 350°F for about 45 minutes or until the loaves are golden and sound hollow when tapped. Turn out of the pans and cool on wire racks. Makes 2 or 3 loaves.

SWEET CARROT BREAD

•

A pretty bread and good enough to eat plain. For a potluck, you could cut thin slices and make lots of little cream cheese sandwiches to arrange on a plate.

1 package (1 scant tablespoon) dry yeast	½ teaspoon grated nutmeg
1 cup warm water	1 teaspoon ground cinnamon
½ cup vegetable oil	1 teaspoon ground ginger
½ cup sugar	½ cup raisins
1½ cups grated carrots	½ cup sunflower seeds (optional)
1 egg	3½ cups unbleached flour
1 teaspoon salt	Honey wash (1 tablespoon honey
1 cup graham or whole wheat flour	mixed with 1 teaspoon water)

*I*n a large bowl, sprinkle the yeast over the warm water. While the yeast dissolves, mix together the oil, sugar, carrots, egg, and salt. Stir the carrot mixture into the dissolved yeast and beat in the graham or whole wheat flour, nutmeg, cinnamon, ginger, raisins, and sunflower seeds if desired. Gradually add the unbleached flour until a soft dough forms. Turn out onto a floured board and knead lightly. (Do not add too much flour.) Place the dough in a greased bowl, turn so the greased side is up, cover, and let rise until doubled, about 1 hour. Punch down and let rest for 10 minutes. Divide the dough in half and shape into 2 loaves, then place in greased bread pans. Begin preheating the oven to 400°F while the dough rises in the pans for about 10 minutes. Brush the tops lightly with the honey wash and bake for 15 minutes at 400°F, then lower the heat to 375°F and bake until done, about 35 minutes longer. The loaves will be golden and sound hollow when tapped. Turn out of the pans and cool on wire racks. Makes 2 loaves.

MILLIE NELSON'S
DINNER ROLLS

•

I interviewed Millie Nelson, then of Goffstown, New Hampshire, for *Yankee* magazine's "Great New England Cooks" series in 1979. At that time Mrs. Nelson said, "These rolls are my own recipe, and I've been making them for years. I must have given away thousands of them. The recipe makes about nine dozen, but you can make fewer rolls and use the rest of the dough for bread." Mrs. Nelson was an inspiring cook who did all of her baking in an Irish wood stove. She believed bread dough should be stirred with a wooden spoon and in one direction only. I make these rolls for special dinners and usually give some away and freeze some. If the quantity seems daunting, cut the recipe in half. But once you taste them, you'll wish you had made more.

—S.P.

2 packages (2 scant tablespoons) dry yeast	*13 cups unbleached flour (approximately)*
½ cup warm water	*2 eggs, slightly beaten*
5 cups milk	*1 cup butter, melted*
1 cup sugar	*1 cup butter, at room temperature*
1 tablespoon salt	

$\mathcal{D}$issolve the yeast in the warm water in a large bowl. Heat the milk to about 100°F (body temperature) and add to the yeast along with the sugar and salt. Gradually stir in 7 cups of the flour, using a wooden spoon and stirring in one direction only for 150 strokes. Add the beaten eggs and melted shortening. Stir well, then add the remaining flour a cup at a time, until you have a soft, sticky dough. Cover the bowl with a damp towel and let rise until doubled, about 1 hour. Punch down and turn out onto a floured board to rest for 10 minutes. Add a small amount of flour if necessary, just enough to enable you to handle the dough. Take about a quarter of the dough and roll out to ¼ inch thick. Spread with the soft butter, using a spatula. Cut into wedges about 3 inches long and 1 to 1½ inches at the short end. Roll up, starting at the short end. (What Mrs. Nelson did, and it's more fun, is to hold a wedge by the short end and twirl until the point wraps itself around. Once you get the hang of it, it goes quickly.) Place the rolls on greased cookie sheets, about 36 rolls to a sheet. Let rise until doubled, then bake in a preheated oven at 400°F until golden. Cool on wire racks. Makes about 9 dozen.

WHOLE WHEAT-PUMPKIN
ROLLS

.

1 package (1 scant tablespoon)
 dry yeast
½ cup warm water
1 teaspoon salt
½ teaspoon freshly grated nutmeg
2 tablespoons vegetable oil or
 melted butter
2 tablespoons honey

1 egg, separated
½ cup canned or mashed
 pumpkin
1 cup whole wheat flour
2 cups unbleached flour
Egg wash (yolk of separated egg
 beaten with 2 teaspoons milk)
¼ cup sesame seeds for topping

Sprinkle the yeast over the warm water in a large mixing bowl. When the yeast is dissolved, add the salt, nutmeg, oil or butter, honey, egg white, pumpkin, and whole wheat flour. Beat until well blended. Gradually add the unbleached flour until you have a soft dough. Knead the dough on a floured board until smooth and elastic. Place in a greased bowl and turn so the greased side is up. Cover and let rise until double, about 45 minutes. Punch down, roll into an 8-by-15-inch rectangle, and cut into 15 strips each 8 by 1 inch. Roll up each strip and tuck the end under. (You could also shape the dough in other ways; try to come out with about 15 rolls.) Place the rolls on a greased cookie sheet, allowing about 2 inches between rolls. Let rise, uncovered, until nearly doubled, about 45 minutes. Brush with the egg wash and sprinkle with the sesame seeds. Bake in a preheated oven at 375°F for about 20 minutes, until the rolls are golden brown and sound hollow when tapped. Serve warm or reheat later in foil for a few minutes in a hot oven. Makes 15 dinner rolls.

BUTTERMILK CORN BREAD

·

I usually bake this in a large quiche pan and cut it into wedges. It's quite heavenly right out of the oven, slathered with butter. Serve it with chowder, baked beans, or just by itself.

—S.P.

*1 cup graham or whole wheat
flour
1 cup cornmeal
2 teaspoons baking powder
1 teaspoon baking soda*

*½ teaspoon salt
1⅓ cups buttermilk
2 eggs
¼ cup vegetable oil
¼ cup brown sugar*

Combine the flour, cornmeal, baking powder, baking soda, and salt in a medium bowl. In a separate bowl, whisk together the buttermilk, eggs, oil, and brown sugar until smooth. Add the buttermilk mixture to the flour mixture and stir just until blended. Pour into a greased quiche pan or 9-inch-square baking pan and bake in a preheated oven at 400°F for about 20 minutes, until golden brown and solid in the center. Serve warm.

TENNESSEE CORN BREAD

·

Celeste Hewson, Gordon's sister, got this from Grace Jones of Burwood, Tennessee. It makes a loaf rather than a flat pan.

*¼ cup shortening
3 cups cornmeal
1 cup flour
½ cup sugar*

*1 teaspoon salt
1 teaspoon baking soda
1 teaspoon baking powder
2¾ cups buttermilk*

$\mathcal{P}$reheat the oven to 325°F and place the shortening in a loaf pan in the oven until the shortening is melted. Meanwhile, sift the cornmeal, flour, sugar, salt, baking soda, and baking powder in a medium bowl. Pour the melted shortening and buttermilk into the cornmeal mixture and stir just until blended. Pour the batter back into the loaf pan and bake for 1 hour at 325°F.

ZUCCHINI BREAD

•

What would summer be without zucchinis the size of rolling pins running amok? Here's one way to use them up, courtesy of Susan's mother, Margaret Mahnke. This makes two loaves—freeze one and save it for a rainy day. Lots of folks grate up any extra zukes and freeze them in one-cup portions to use later in breads and soups. No need to peel before grating; just remove the stem ends and any blemishes.

3 eggs
2 cups sugar
1 cup vegetable oil
2 cups grated zucchini
2 teaspoons vanilla
1 tablespoon grated orange rind
3 cups flour

1 teaspoon salt
1 teaspoon baking soda
½ teaspoon baking powder
2 teaspoons ground cinnamon
2 teaspoons ground ginger
1 cup chopped walnuts

$\mathcal{B}$eat the eggs in a large bowl and add the sugar, oil, zucchini, vanilla, and orange rind. Stir until well blended. Sift together the flour, salt, baking soda, baking powder, cinnamon, and ginger. Add to the zucchini mixture and stir until well mixed. Stir in the walnuts. Pour into 2 greased 9-by-5-inch loaf pans and bake in a preheated oven at 350°F for about 1 hour or until the bread tests done. Cool in the pans for about 10 minutes, then gently turn out onto wire racks to finish cooling. Makes 2 loaves.

PINEAPPLE-PECAN BREAD

·

½ cup butter, at room
   temperature
1 cup sugar
2 eggs
2 cups flour

1 teaspoon baking powder
¼ teaspoon salt
1 cup drained crushed pineapple
   (1 small can)
½ cup chopped pecans

Cream the butter and sugar and add the eggs one at a time, beating until the mixture is light. Whisk the flour, baking powder, and salt together and add to the butter mixture alternately with the pineapple. Fold in the nuts. Pour into a greased and floured loaf pan (either 9-by-5-inch or 8-by-4-inch) and bake in a preheated oven at 350°F for 50 to 60 minutes, until the loaf tests done. Cool in the pan for 10 minutes before removing to a wire rack. Cool before slicing.

MAPLE-NUT LOAF

·

Carole Thomas Downing, who gave us the recipe, earned spending money as a child by making this bread and selling it door-to-door in her neighborhood. It goes well with a meal and is sweet enough to pass as a dessert (perhaps with a scoop of vanilla ice cream on the side).

2 cups unbleached flour
¾ cup whole wheat flour
½ cup sugar
1 tablespoon baking powder
½ teaspoon salt
1 egg, beaten

1 cup milk
¾ teaspoon maple flavoring
½ cup maple syrup
1½ cups coarsely chopped
   walnuts

Combine the flour, sugar, baking powder, and salt in a large bowl. In a medium bowl, beat the egg, milk, maple flavoring, and syrup until smooth. Add the maple mixture to the flour mixture and stir until well mixed. Stir in the nuts. Pour into 1 large (either 9-by-5-inch or 8-by-4-inch) or 2 smaller 6-by-3-inch greased loaf pans. Let stand for 20 minutes, then bake in a preheated oven at 350°F for about 1 hour, until the bread tests done. Cool in the pan for 5 minutes, then turn out onto a wire rack.

RHUBARB-NUT BREAD WITH STREUSEL TOPPING

·

This bread is tart and sweet all at once, and delicious spread with butter or cream cheese.

1½ cups brown sugar
⅔ cup vegetable oil
2 eggs
1 teaspoon baking soda
1 teaspoon salt
1 teaspoon vanilla

1 cup soured milk (2 tablespoons lemon juice plus milk to equal 1 cup)
2½ cups flour
1½ cups diced rhubarb
¾ cup chopped nuts

STREUSEL TOPPING
½ cup butter, at room temperature
½ cup flour

½ cup brown sugar
½ cup finely chopped nuts
1 teaspoon ground cinnamon

In a large bowl, beat the brown sugar, oil, and eggs until smooth. In a separate bowl, mix the baking soda, salt, vanilla, and soured milk. Add to the brown sugar mixture. Stir in the flour, rhubarb, and nuts. Pour into 2 greased loaf pans (either 9-by-5-inch or 8-by-4-inch).

Place the streusel ingredients in a small bowl and mix well with a fork or your fingertips. Sprinkle over the top of the batter. Bake in a preheated oven at 350°F for 1 hour or until the bread tests done.

Cooking
for
Friends

180

THE QUICK BROWN LOAF

■

Born to be served with baked beans. You can make twelve to fifteen muffins instead of one large loaf. Pour the batter into greased muffin tins and bake for twenty to twenty-five minutes.

1 cup unbleached flour
2 cups whole wheat flour
2 teaspoons baking soda
1 teaspoon salt
1 cup brown sugar

¼ cup molasses
1½ cups buttermilk
3 tablespoons butter, melted
1 egg, beaten

Stir the flour, baking soda, and salt together in a large bowl. In a medium bowl, beat the brown sugar, molasses, buttermilk, melted butter, and egg until smooth. Stir the liquid mixture into the flour mixture and beat until smooth. Pour into a greased 9-by-5-inch loaf pan and let stand for 20 minutes, then bake in a preheated oven at 350°F for 45 minutes, until the bread tests done. Cool in the pan for a few minutes, then turn onto a serving plate or wire rack.

BRAN MUFFINS WITH FRUIT

■

Sounds like more fiber than a textile mill, but they're good, really.

2 cups bran flakes cereal
1½ cups milk
2 eggs
½ cup vegetable oil
2 cups flour
½ cup sugar

2 tablespoons baking powder
½ teaspoon salt
1 large apple, peeled and chopped
½ cup chopped dried apricots
½ cup raisins

Combine the bran flakes and milk in a large bowl and stir until the cereal is softened. Add the eggs and oil and mix well. Whisk together the flour, sugar, baking powder, and salt and add to the liquid mixture, stirring just until moistened. Add the apple, apricots, and raisins and stir until the fruit is distributed. Spoon the batter into 15 to 18 greased muffin cups and bake in a preheated oven at 375°F for about 25 minutes, until the muffins test done. Makes 15 to 18 muffins.

SUGAR-DIPPED
APPLESAUCE MUFFINS

·

I bake these in the little muffin cups that measure about one and three-quarter inches top diameter. If, like me, you only own two of the little twelve-unit tins and thus can make only twenty-four bitty muffins, use the rest of the batter to make five or six regular size muffins.

—S.P.

½ cup butter, at room
  temperature
½ cup sugar
2 eggs
¾ cup applesauce
1¾ cups flour

1 tablespoon baking powder
½ teaspoon salt
¼ cup butter, melted
½ cup sugar mixed with
  ½ teaspoon cinnamon

Combine the softened butter and sugar. Beat in the eggs until the mixture is light, then stir in the applesauce. Whisk together the flour, baking powder, and salt and add to the butter-sugar mixture, stirring only until the flour is moistened. Spoon the batter into 36 greased mini-muffin cups and bake in a preheated oven at 425°F for about 15 minutes. While the muffins are still warm, dip the tops in the melted butter and then into the cinnamon sugar. Serve warm if possible. Makes 36 mini-muffins.

BEST BLUEBERRY MUFFINS

·

Our children love to graze among the blueberry bushes when the berries are ripe, but we can usually manage to pick a pint, enough for a good-sized batch of muffins. Ripe berries are completely blue, with a silver haze. Berries with a reddish tinge are unripe. (Got that, Spencer?)

6 tablespoons butter, at room temperature	*½ teaspoon salt*
	2 teaspoons baking powder
1 cup sugar	*½ cup milk*
2 eggs	*1 pint blueberries, divided*
2 cups flour	*1 tablespoon sugar*

Cream the butter and sugar until light. Add the eggs and beat well. Whisk the flour, salt, and baking powder together and add to the butter mixture alternately with the milk to make a thick batter. Crush ½ cup of the blueberries and mix into the batter, then fold in the remaining whole berries. Spoon into 16 greased muffin cups and sprinkle the sugar over the batter. Bake in a preheated oven at 375°F for about 25 minutes, until golden brown. Cool in the muffin tins for 5 minutes, then remove to a wire rack or serving plate. Makes 16 muffins.

GRANDMA'S FRUIT BREAD

·

Susan Lord, granddaughter of the author of this recipe, wrote, "My mother's mother was famous for her coffee parties—a family institution that taught me cooking was just another word for love."

1 cup snipped dried apricots

1½ cups sugar

½ cup butter, at room
  temperature

4 eggs

4 cups sifted flour

2 tablespoons baking powder

1 teaspoon salt

2 cups milk

1 cup snipped prunes

1 cup chopped walnuts

Cover the apricots with water and let stand for 5 minutes, then drain. In a mixer bowl, cream the sugar and butter. Add the eggs and beat until light. Sift together the flour, baking powder, and salt. Add the dry ingredients alternately with the milk to the butter mixture, beating well after each addition. Stir in the apricots, prunes, and walnuts.

Pour into 2 greased and floured 9-by-5-inch bread pans. Bake in a preheated oven at 350°F for 1 hour. Cool in the pans for 10 minutes, then remove to wire racks and let cool completely. Wrap and store overnight for best slicing. Makes 2 loaves.

OATMEAL-DATE MUFFINS

·

Don't worry if these muffins come out of the oven with flat tops; they just do that.

1 cup flour

2 teaspoons baking powder

½ teaspoon baking soda

½ teaspoon salt

1 cup old-fashioned rolled oats

1 cup buttermilk

½ cup brown sugar

1 egg, beaten

½ cup butter, melted, or ½ cup
  vegetable oil

½ cup chopped dates

Whisk the flour, baking powder, baking soda, and salt together in a medium bowl. In a large bowl, soak the oats in the buttermilk. Add the brown sugar, egg, and butter or oil. Beat until blended. Add the dates to the liquid mixture. Add the flour mixture to the liquid mixture and stir only enough to moisten. Spoon into 12 greased muffin cups and bake in a preheated oven at 375°F for about 25 minutes, until golden brown. Makes 12 muffins.

Ten

DESSERTS

■

As you orbit in your various social circles, you may well attend (or host) a dessert potluck—a gathering of friends, perhaps after the supper hour, with each person bearing a dessert. No salads, no quiches, no beans—just desserts. This provides a chance to indulge your sweet tooth while socializing and perhaps wheedling a few recipes out of good bakers.

We have never been to a potluck supper that didn't include at least a couple of good desserts. But be warned by what happened to one friend who arrived at a potluck to find not a single dessert—and, worst of all, everyone had brought coleslaw!

To avoid such an awkward and unhappy experience, we offer the following ideas for desserts, starting with old faithful chocolate cake (several variations) and proceeding through coffee cakes and gingerbreads, pies, kuchens and tortes, baklava, cookies and tea cakes, bars (or maybe you call them squares), and, circling back to chocolate, fudge.

MIDNIGHT CHOCOLATE
CAKE

•

1 cup unsweetened cocoa

2 cups boiling water

3 cups flour

1 teaspoon salt

2 teaspoons baking soda

2 teaspoons baking powder

1 cup butter, at room temperature

2½ cups sugar

4 eggs

2 teaspoons vanilla

Whisk the cocoa into the boiling water and set aside. Sift the flour, salt, baking soda, and baking powder together. In a large bowl or heavy-duty mixer, cream the butter and sugar until light. Add the eggs one at a time and beat well. Add the vanilla. Add a third of the dry ingredients, then a third of the cocoa mixture. Repeat until all the ingredients are incorporated and the batter is smooth. Pour into a greased and floured 9-by-13-inch pan. Bake in a preheated oven at 350°F for 25 to 30 minutes, until the cake tests done. Cool before frosting.

A chocolate frosting, such as the Fudge Frosting (page 192), makes this cake a chocolate lover's dream. However, we confess to a fondness for "white" frosting on chocolate cake and often make a simple confectioners sugar icing using ¼ cup softened butter, 2½ cups confectioners sugar, 1 teaspoon vanilla, and enough hot water to achieve the proper consistency. Beat everything until smooth.

CHOCOLATE BANANA
CAKE

■

Our friend Steve Zakon, who makes both cooking and contra dance calling look easy, gave us this recipe, which he got from his father, who took up baking when he retired. It makes a nice, moist nine-by-nine-inch cake or about ten cupcakes.

9 tablespoons margarine, at room
  temperature
1¼ cups sugar
2 eggs
½ cup soured milk (1½ teaspoons
  lemon juice plus milk to equal
  ½ cup)

1 cup mashed ripe bananas
  (2 medium or 3 small)
1 cup flour
½ cup unsweetened cocoa, sifted
¼ teaspoon salt
1 teaspoon baking soda

Cream the margarine and sugar. Beat in the eggs, soured milk, and bananas. Stir together the flour, cocoa, salt, and baking soda. Add the flour mixture to the egg mixture and beat well. Pour into a greased and floured 9-by-9-inch pan and bake in a preheated oven at 350°F for about 35 minutes, until the cake tests done.

LINDY'S CHOCOLATE-
MAYONNAISE CAKE

·

We got the recipe for this moist chocolate cake from our friend Lindy Black, who lives in Nelson and is the minister of the Nelson Congregational Church.

2 cups flour
1½ teaspoons baking soda
1½ teaspoons baking powder
⅓ cup unsweetened cocoa

1 cup sugar
¾ cup mayonnaise
1 cup cold water
2 teaspoons vanilla

In a medium bowl, blend the flour, baking soda, and baking powder. In a separate bowl, blend the sugar, mayonnaise, water, and vanilla. Gradually add the flour mixture and beat well. Pour into a greased 9-by-13-inch cake pan. Bake in a preheated oven at 375°F for about 25 minutes, until the cake tests done. Cool before frosting.

MISSISSIPPI MUD CAKE

—

•

Jane Miller gave us this recipe, a favorite in her family. "Sindee Ernst brought it to our house one spring," Jane said, "and at first we thought she had scraped it up off the road! Since then, we make it each mud season. It *won't* get us down."

2 cups flour
1 teaspoon baking soda
Dash of salt
5 squares baking chocolate
1 cup butter
1¾ cups good brewed coffee

¼ cup bourbon
2½ cups sugar
2 eggs, slightly beaten
1 teaspoon vanilla
Cocoa for dusting pan

Sift together the flour, baking soda, and salt. In a double boiler over simmering water, melt and mix together the chocolate, butter, coffee, and bourbon. Add the sugar to the melted chocolate-butter mixture, then cool for 3 minutes. Put the chocolate-butter mixture in a mixing bowl and add the flour mixture ½ cup at a time until it is incorporated. Beat at medium speed for 1 minute. Add the eggs and vanilla and beat until smooth. Grease a 10-inch tube pan and dust with cocoa, then pour the batter into the pan. Bake in a preheated oven at 275°F for 1½ hours. Cool in the pan for 15 minutes before removing. Serve in thin slices with whipped cream.

NOTE This is a moist cake and if you must transport it any distance, let it cool in the pan and turn out onto a platter at your destination.

THIRTY-MINUTE CHOCOLATE CAKE

■

We got this recipe from Jean deLongchamp, Susan's colleague at work, who makes it for office birthday parties. It takes about thirty minutes to make, from mixing to frosting.

2 cups flour
2 cups sugar
½ cup vegetable shortening
½ cup butter
3½ tablespoons unsweetened
 cocoa
1 cup water

3 eggs
1 teaspoon baking soda
Dash of salt
½ cup buttermilk or soured milk
 (1½ teaspoons lemon juice plus
 milk to equal ½ cup)
1 teaspoon vanilla

FROSTING
½ cup butter
4 tablespoons unsweetened cocoa
⅓ cup milk
3½ cups sifted confectioners sugar

Dash of salt
1 teaspoon vanilla
1 cup chopped nuts

Mix the flour and sugar together in a large bowl. Combine the shortening, butter, cocoa, and water in a saucepan and bring to a boil. Pour over the flour mixture and blend well. Stir in the eggs, baking soda, salt, buttermilk or soured milk, and vanilla and beat well. Bake in a greased 9-by-13-inch pan in a preheated oven at 375°F for 20 to 25 minutes, until the cake tests done.

Five minutes before the cake comes out of the oven, prepare the frosting. Bring the butter, cocoa, and milk to a boil in a medium saucepan. Add the sugar, salt, vanilla, and nuts and beat well. Pour the frosting over the hot cake. Cool before serving.

CHOCOLATE ZUCCHINI
CAKE

∎

For the truly desperate parent, a way to get the kids to eat their vegetables.

2½ cups flour
½ cup unsweetened cocoa
½ teaspoon salt
2½ teaspoons baking powder
1½ teaspoons baking soda
1 teaspoon ground cinnamon
¾ cup butter or margarine (or a
  combination), at room
  temperature
2 cups sugar

3 eggs
2 cups shredded zucchini (cut off
  ends, but do not peel before
  shredding)
1 teaspoon vanilla
1 tablespoon grated orange peel
¼ cup milk
1 cup chopped walnuts
Confectioners sugar for dusting
  cake (optional)

Sift together the flour, cocoa, salt, baking powder, baking soda, and cinnamon. In a large bowl, cream the butter or margarine and the sugar until smooth. Add the eggs one at a time, beating well with each addition. Squeeze the moisture out of the shredded zucchini and add to the egg mixture along with the vanilla and orange peel. Stir in the dry ingredients and milk. Beat well. Stir in the walnuts. Bake in a greased and floured 10-inch tube or bundt pan in a preheated oven at 350°F for 55 to 60 minutes. Test for doneness before removing from the oven. Cool in the pan on a wire rack for 15 minutes, then remove from the pan and finish cooling. Dust with confectioners sugar if desired; no other frosting is required.

CHOCOLATE MATZOH
LAYER CAKE

•

We learned to make this from our friend Steve Zakon, whose mother traditionally makes it at Passover. It makes a spectacular presentation for a special occasion. Because it is precarious to transport, it is a good choice when hosting a potluck, or to bring along if you are traveling a short distance on smooth roads.

CHOCOLATE FILLING

6 ounces bittersweet chocolate	13⅓ tablespoons margarine
5 eggs, separated	1⅔ cups superfine sugar
Sweet wine (Concord grape wine or other)	8 unbroken egg matzohs
	½ cup chopped walnuts

To make the filling, melt the chocolate over hot water or very low heat. Set aside. Beat the egg whites until stiff. Cream the margarine and sugar until light and add the egg yolks one at a time, beating well after each addition. Fold in the melted chocolate, then fold in the egg whites.

To assemble, pour the wine into a flat square pan larger than the matzoh. Dip 1 matzoh in the wine, let the excess run off, and place on a flat plate. Spread with 3 rounded tablespoons (about ¼ cup) filling. Repeat the dipping and layering until all 8 matzohs are used. Cover the top and sides with the remaining chocolate filling. Sprinkle the top with the nuts. Cover and refrigerate for 24 hours, making sure the cover does not touch the cake. Slice with a sharp knife to serve.

FUDGE FROSTING

—— ■

3 squares unsweetened baking
  chocolate
¼ cup butter, at room
  temperature

3 cups confectioners sugar, sifted
  after measuring
¼ cup light cream
2 teaspoons vanilla

Melt the chocolate and butter together in a small, heavy pan over
very low heat. In a medium bowl, beat the sugar, cream, and
vanilla together with an electric mixer until smooth. Add the cooled
chocolate mixture gradually and beat at high speed. Add more sugar
if the frosting seems runny, or more cream if it is too stiff.

BARBARA'S MARSHMALLOW-
FUDGE FROSTING

—— ■

Our neighbor, Barbara Fraser, who is a fine cook and whose
chickens supply us with good brown eggs, uses this frosting on a
cake similar to Lindy's Chocolate-Mayonnaise Cake (page 187).

¼ cup water
3 squares unsweetened baking
  chocolate
2 tablespoons butter

12 large marshmallows, cut up
½ teaspoon salt
2 cups confectioners sugar
1 teaspoon vanilla

Over low heat, stir the water, chocolate, butter, marshmallows,
and salt until soft and blended. Add the sugar and vanilla. Add
a few drops of hot water if the frosting is too stiff.

PRUNE CAKE

•

We got this recipe from Gail Burkhardt, a schoolteacher and folk dancer. She claims it will keep an entire Morris team happy for a weekend.

1½ cups cut-up prunes
1 cup hot water
2 cups flour
½ teaspoon salt
1 teaspoon ground cinnamon
½ teaspoon ground nutmeg
½ teaspoon ground cloves

1¼ teaspoons baking soda
½ cup vegetable oil
2 eggs
1¼ cups sugar
1 cup nuts
½ cup raisins

Simmer the prunes in the hot water for 5 minutes. Sift together the flour, salt, cinnamon, nutmeg, cloves, and baking soda. Add the hot prune mixture, oil, eggs, and sugar to the flour mixture. Beat for 1 minute. Stir in the nuts and raisins. Pour into a greased and floured 9-by-13-inch pan and bake in a preheated oven at 350°F for 35 to 40 minutes, until the cake tests done. Cool in the pan on a wire rack.

SPICY CARROT CAKE

•

from Jenny Coffin

BRATTLEBORO, VERMONT

2 cups sugar
1 cup vegetable oil
3 eggs
2 cups flour
½ teaspoon salt
1 teaspoon baking soda
1 teaspoon ground cinnamon

½ teaspoon ground nutmeg
½ teaspoon ground cloves
1 cup chopped walnuts or pecans
1 cup shredded carrots
One 8-ounce can crushed
   pineapple, drained

In a large bowl, combine the sugar, oil, and eggs and beat well. Sift together the flour, salt, baking soda, cinnamon, nutmeg, and cloves and add to the egg mixture. Mix well. Fold in the nuts, carrots, and pineapple. Pour into a greased 9-by-13-inch pan and bake in a preheated oven at 350°F for about 40 minutes, until the cake tests done. Cool completely in the pan on a wire rack before frosting. Frost with Cream Cheese Frosting (below).

CREAM CHEESE FROSTING

•

6 ounces cream cheese, at room
   temperature
¼ cup butter, at room
   temperature

2 cups confectioners sugar
1 teaspoon vanilla
Dash of salt

*B*eat the cream cheese and butter until creamy. Add the sugar, vanilla, and salt and beat until smooth. If the frosting is too stiff, add a few drops of hot water. This frosting may also be made in the food processor, using the plastic blade: Combine all the ingredients and whirr until smooth.

CARDAMOM CAKE

•

This cake tastes even better the day after baking, when the flavors have mellowed together.

3⅓ cups flour
2½ teaspoons baking powder
¼ teaspoon salt
1½ teaspoons ground cardamom
½ teaspoon ground allspice
2 cups sugar
1 cup butter, at room temperature
2 eggs

1 teaspoon almond extract
1 tablespoon grated orange rind
2 teaspoons grated lemon rind
2 tablespoons orange juice
1 cup half-and-half
Confectioners sugar for dusting
  cake (optional)

*S*ift the flour with the baking powder, salt, cardamom, and all-spice. In a large bowl, cream the sugar and butter and beat until light. Add the eggs, almond extract, and orange and lemon rinds. Beat well. Combine the orange juice and half-and-half in a small bowl. Alternately add the dry ingredients and the half-and-half mixture to the egg mixture, beating well after each addition. Spread the batter in a greased 9-by-13-inch pan. Bake in a preheated oven at 350°F for about 40 minutes, until the cake tests done. Cool in the pan on a wire rack. When completely cool, cover the pan with foil or plastic wrap. If desired, dust with confectioners sugar before serving; no other frosting is required.

CARROT AND APPLE CAKE

•

Gordon's sister, Celeste Hewson, makes this for potlucks in Thompson Station, Tennessee. Make it a day ahead for best taste.

1 cup butter, at room temperature
1 cup sugar
1 teaspoon ground cinnamon
½ teaspoon ground nutmeg
2 teaspoons grated orange rind
4 eggs
2 cups grated carrots

1 large tart apple, peeled and
   diced
½ cup chopped walnuts or pecans
⅔ cup chopped raisins
2½ cups flour
1 tablespoon baking powder
⅓ cup warm water

Cream the butter and sugar. Add the spices and orange rind. Beat in the eggs one at a time. Stir in the carrots, apple, nuts, and raisins. Sift the flour and baking powder. Add to the creamed mixture with the water. Stir to blend, but do not beat. Pour into a greased 9-by-13-inch pan. Bake in a preheated oven at 350°F for 45 to 55 minutes. Cool in the pan on a wire rack.

SPICED APPLESAUCE CAKE

•

½ cup butter or margarine, at
   room temperature
¾ cup sugar
1 teaspoon ground cinnamon
½ teaspoon ground allspice
1 egg
1 teaspoon baking soda

1 cup applesauce
2 cups flour
½ teaspoon salt
2 teaspoons brandy or vanilla
1 cup golden raisins
Confectioners sugar for dusting
   cake

Cream the butter or margarine and the sugar until fluffy. Beat in the cinnamon, allspice, and egg. Dissolve the baking soda in the applesauce and add to the egg mixture. Blend in the flour and salt. Add the brandy or vanilla and the raisins and mix well. Pour into a greased 9-inch bundt pan. Bake in a preheated oven at 350°F for 55 to 60 minutes, until the cake tests done. Cool for 15 minutes in the pan on a wire rack, then remove from the pan and finish cooling. Dust with confectioners sugar or drizzle with a thin confectioners sugar icing (page 186).

FRESH APPLE CAKE

■

This tastes especially wonderful in the fall, when new apples are tart and juicy and cider is sweet and thick.

¾ cup butter, at room
  temperature
2 cups sugar
2 eggs
2 cups flour
1 teaspoon baking powder
1 teaspoon baking soda
½ teaspoon ground cinnamon

¼ teaspoon salt
3 tablespoons apple cider
2 cups peeled and chopped apples
1 cup chopped walnuts
1 cup raisins
⅓ cup coconut
1 tablespoon sugar

Cream the butter and 2 cups sugar. Add the eggs one at a time. Mix well. Sift the flour with the baking powder, baking soda, cinnamon, and salt and add to the egg mixture alternately with the cider. Mix well. Fold in the apples, walnuts, raisins, and coconut. The batter will be thick. Pour into a greased 9-by-13-inch pan, sprinkle with the 1 tablespoon sugar, and bake in a preheated oven at 350°F for 40 to 50 minutes. Cool pan on a rack.

PUMPKIN-SPICE CAKE

■

This makes two beautiful nine-inch layers. If you hesitate at the thought of transporting a frosted layer cake to a potluck, consider wrapping the layers, unfrosted, bringing the frosting along in a bowl, and assembling the cake on the spot.

1½ cups corn oil	½ teaspoon salt
4 large eggs	1 tablespoon baking soda
2 teaspoons vanilla	2 teaspoons ground cinnamon
3 tablespoons rum or orange juice	½ teaspoon ground allspice
One 16-ounce can pumpkin (about 2 cups)	¼ teaspoon ground mace
	½ teaspoon ground nutmeg
3 cups flour	2 teaspoons ground ginger
3 cups sugar	1 cup chopped pecans

GINGER CREAM CHEESE FROSTING

8 ounces cream cheese, at room temperature	3½ cups confectioners sugar
	1 tablespoon lemon juice
6 tablespoons butter, at room temperature	2 tablespoons finely chopped crystallized ginger

In a large bowl, combine the oil, eggs, vanilla, rum or orange juice, and pumpkin. Beat well. Place the flour, sugar, salt, baking soda, cinnamon, allspice, mace, nutmeg, and ginger in another large bowl and whisk to blend. Fold the flour mixture slowly into the pumpkin mixture until well incorporated. Stir in the pecans. Divide the batter between 2 greased and floured 9-inch cake pans. Bake in a preheated oven at 350°F for about 45 minutes, until the cake tests done. Cool in the pans on wire racks. Frost when completely cool.

Beat the cream cheese and butter. Sift in the confectioners sugar and whip until fluffy. Stir in the lemon juice and fold in the crystallized ginger. Spread the icing thinly on the bottom cake layer. Set the second layer on top and frost the sides and then the top of the cake.

WESTHAVEN CAKE

•

Susan got this recipe in the summer of 1969 from JoAnne Kraus, who brought it to office get-togethers at the Kohler Company, Kohler, Wisconsin. The cake is moist and the combination of dates and chocolate is quite tasty. The chocolate and nut topping takes the place of frosting.

One 7-ounce package chopped dates (about 1 cup)
1 cup hot water
1¾ cups flour
1 teaspoon baking soda
½ teaspoon salt
½ cup butter or margarine, at room temperature

1 cup sugar
1 teaspoon vanilla
2 eggs
1 cup semisweet chocolate chips
½ cup chopped pecans

Combine the dates and water in a small saucepan and bring to a boil. Let cool. Drain the dates, saving the water. Sift the flour with the baking soda and salt. Cream the shortening and sugar in a large bowl. Add the vanilla. Add the eggs to the shortening mixture one at a time, beating after each addition. Alternately add the flour mixture and the date water, and mix until the batter is smooth. Stir in the dates. Pour the batter into a greased 9-by-13-inch pan. Sprinkle the chocolate chips and nuts over the top of the batter. Bake in a preheated oven at 350°F for about 35 minutes, until the cake tests done. Cool pan on a rack.

RHUBARB CAKE

■

This simple cake takes advantage of our ample rhubarb crop in June and July.

½ cup butter, at room
  temperature
1½ cups brown sugar
1 egg
1 teaspoon vanilla
2 cups flour

1 teaspoon baking soda
1 cup buttermilk
2 cups diced rhubarb
2 tablespoons sugar
1 teaspoon ground cinnamon
  (or to taste)

Cream the butter and brown sugar. Add the egg and vanilla and beat until smooth. Combine the flour and baking soda. Add to the egg mixture alternately with the buttermilk until the flour is incorporated. Fold in the rhubarb. Pour into a greased 9-by-13-inch pan. Combine the sugar and cinnamon and sprinkle evenly over the batter. Bake in a preheated oven at 350°F for about 45 minutes, until the cake tests done. Cool in the pan on a wire rack.

MOM'S SCANDINAVIAN KRINGLE

•

We got this recipe from Susan's mother, Margaret Mahnke. She often makes this, or the Overnight Crunch Coffee Cake (page 203), for weekday-morning card parties with her friends in Sheboygan, Wisconsin.

CRUST
1 cup flour
½ cup butter

2 tablespoons ice water

PUFF TOPPING
1 cup water
½ cup butter
1 cup flour

1 teaspoon almond extract
3 eggs

FROSTING
1 cup confectioners sugar
1 tablespoon butter, at room temperature

½ teaspoon almond extract
2 to 3 tablespoons milk

For the crust, place the flour in a medium bowl. Cut the butter into small pieces and add to the flour. Mix together as for a pie crust. Toss with the ice water. Divide the dough in half and press each half onto a cookie sheet in a strip 12 inches long and 3 inches wide.

For the puff topping, heat the water and butter to boiling in a medium saucepan. Remove from the heat and stir in the flour and almond extract until the mixture is smooth. Add the eggs one at a time and beat. Pour over the strips of crust and bake in a preheated oven at 350°F for 50 to 60 minutes, until golden. Cool on a rack before frosting.

Combine all the frosting ingredients and beat together until smooth. Drizzle over the cooled Kringle.

CRUMB CAKE

·

One of Susan's favorite childhood memories is of her grandmother, Helen Michaels, walking across the field that separated their houses and carrying a warm-from-the-oven Crumb Cake to share. This is Grandma's recipe.

¾ cup butter, at room
  temperature
1½ cups brown sugar
2½ cups flour
1 teaspoon baking soda
1 cup buttermilk or soured milk
  (2 tablespoons lemon juice plus
  milk to equal 1 cup)

1 egg, beaten
1 teaspoon vanilla
Dash of salt

Combine the butter, brown sugar, and flour in a large bowl and work together until the mixture forms fine crumbs. Remove 1 cupful of the mixture and reserve for the topping. Dissolve the baking soda in the buttermilk or soured milk and add it to the remaining flour mixture along with the egg, vanilla, and salt. Mix until well blended. Pour into a greased 9-by-13-inch pan, or two 8-inch round cake pans. Sprinkle the reserved topping mixture over the batter. Bake in a preheated oven at 350°F for 25 to 30 minutes, until golden brown.

OVERNIGHT CRUNCH COFFEE CAKE

·

This coffee cake can be completely mixed twelve hours ahead of time and baked just before a gathering.

2 cups sifted flour
1 teaspoon baking powder
1 teaspoon baking soda
1 teaspoon ground cinnamon
½ teaspoon salt
⅔ cup butter or margarine, at room temperature

1 cup sugar
½ cup brown sugar
2 eggs
1 cup buttermilk

TOPPING

½ cup brown sugar
½ cup chopped walnuts

½ teaspoon ground cinnamon
¼ teaspoon ground nutmeg

Sift the flour, baking powder, baking soda, cinnamon, and salt together. In a large bowl, cream the butter or margarine, sugar, and brown sugar until fluffy. Add the eggs to the butter mixture one at a time, beating after each addition. Add the dry ingredients alternately with the buttermilk. Spread in a greased and floured 9-by-13-inch pan.

With a fork, combine the topping ingredients in a small bowl and sprinkle over the batter. Refrigerate overnight or for 12 hours. Bake on a rack in a preheated oven at 350°F for 45 minutes.

SOUR CREAM
COFFEE CAKE

■

Some recipes get around: We got this one several years ago from our friend Deborah Navas, who got it years before that from her college roommate's mother.

1½ cups flour
1½ teaspoons baking powder
½ teaspoon baking soda
½ teaspoon salt
½ cup butter, at room
  temperature

½ cup sugar
2 eggs
1 teaspoon vanilla
½ cup sour cream

STREUSEL

4 tablespoons brown sugar
4 tablespoons butter
6 tablespoons flour

½ teaspoon ground cinnamon
½ cup finely chopped walnuts

For the cake batter, sift together the flour, baking powder, baking soda, and salt. Cream the butter and sugar until light. Add the eggs and vanilla and mix well. Add the dry ingredients to the butter mixture in several portions alternating with the sour cream.

Mix the streusel ingredients together in a small bowl using a fork or pastry blender. Pour half of the batter into a greased and floured tube or bundt pan. Sprinkle with half of the streusel, then repeat. Bake in a preheated oven at 350°F for about 40 minutes, until the cake tests done. Cool in the pan on a wire rack for 15 minutes before removing to a serving plate.

MAPLE-CRANBERRY COFFEE CAKE

•

Steve Zakon, who dreamed this up, loves to use maple syrup in baking and cooking.

1½ cups cranberries	2 eggs
¼ cup water	2 cups flour
½ cup sugar	1 teaspoon baking powder
½ cup butter, at room temperature	½ teaspoon salt
	½ teaspoon baking soda
¾ cup maple syrup (preferably A-dark amber; it's darker than grade A or fancy)	1 cup sour cream
	⅓ cup chopped walnuts

¼ cup maple syrup	6 tablespoons confectioners sugar

*P*lace the cranberries, water, and sugar in a small saucepan. Bring to a simmer. Remove from the heat as soon as the cranberries begin to split.

In a medium bowl, beat the butter with the ¾ cup syrup, then beat in the eggs. Sift together the flour, baking powder, salt, and baking soda. Mix the dry ingredients alternately with the sour cream into the butter mixture. Fold in the nuts. Spoon in the cranberries, using a slotted spoon to leave the liquid behind in the saucepan. Gently fold the berries into the batter. Pour the batter into a greased and floured bundt pan. Bake in a preheated oven at 350°F for 45 minutes, until the cake tests done. Let cool in the pan for 15 minutes, then remove and set right side up on a serving plate. Let cool completely.

In a small bowl, whisk together the ¼ cup syrup and the confectioners sugar. Drizzle the mixture over the cooled cake.

SOUR CREAM TWISTS

■

Mary Sheldon got this recipe from her mother-in-law. The dough can be mixed the night before, or in the morning for an evening get-together.

4 cups flour	*¼ cup lukewarm water*
1 teaspoon salt	*3 eggs*
1 cup shortening	*1 cup sour cream*
1 package (1 scant tablespoon)	*1 teaspoon vanilla*
dry yeast	*1¼ to 1½ cups sugar*

Combine the flour and salt in a large bowl. Cut in the shortening. Dissolve the yeast in the lukewarm water in a small bowl. In a medium bowl, beat the eggs until well blended. Stir in the sour cream and vanilla and add the yeast mixture. Add the egg mixture to the flour and salt and mix thoroughly. Let the dough rise in the refrigerator for at least 2 hours, or overnight.

Sprinkle a small amount of sugar on a bread board. Place the dough on the sugar, sprinkle the dough lightly with more sugar, fold the dough into the center from 2 sides, and roll the dough out to a square 10 or 12 inches on a side. Sprinkle the dough with more sugar, fold into the center, and roll again. Repeat the folding and rolling 4 times, sprinkling the sugar on the board and dough to prevent sticking. Finally, with the dough rolled out into a square, cut into strips ¾ inch wide and 4 inches long. Twist the strips and place on ungreased cookie sheets, allowing space between the twists. Bake in a preheated oven at 375°F for about 30 minutes, until lightly browned.

PUMPKIN GINGERBREAD
WITH CARAMEL SAUCE

·

Folksinger Deborah McClatchy and her family meet once a month with seven other families (with fourteen children among them) for a potluck meal in their rural Pennsylvania community of Roaring Spring. She improvised this recipe from ingredients on hand, and it has become a favorite. At one meal, to the amusement of those watching, one of her friends poured caramel sauce onto his pot roast, thinking it was gravy. (Turns out, it goes better with the gingerbread.)

GINGERBREAD

½ cup butter, at room
  temperature
½ cup brown sugar
1 egg
⅔ cup molasses
1¾ cups flour

1 teaspoon baking soda
1 teaspoon ground ginger
½ teaspoon ground cinnamon
¼ teaspoon ground allspice
¼ teaspoon ground cloves
⅔ cup mashed pumpkin

CARAMEL SAUCE

½ cup butter
1 cup brown sugar
2 tablespoons light corn syrup

½ cup half-and-half
1 teaspoon vanilla
⅓ cup mashed pumpkin

For the gingerbread, cream the butter and brown sugar, then beat in the egg and molasses. Sift the flour, baking soda, ginger, cinnamon, allspice, and cloves together. Add to the butter mixture alternately with the pumpkin. Pour into a greased 9-inch-square pan and bake in a preheated oven at 350°F for 35 to 40 minutes, until the gingerbread tests done.

For the caramel sauce, melt the butter in a saucepan. Stir in the brown sugar and corn syrup and bring to a boil for 2 minutes. Remove from the heat. Add the half-and-half and vanilla and cool partially. To serve, cut the gingerbread into squares, pour the sauce over the top, and garnish with a dollop of the pumpkin.

MARY'S GINGERBREAD

·

Our friend Mary DesRosiers, a person of many talents (including calling contra dances and simultaneously raising a teenage daughter and twin preschool boys), evolved this recipe from *The Farm Cookbook*.

½ cup oil
1 cup molasses (please, no
  blackstrap)
2 cups flour
2 to 4 teaspoons ground ginger,
  depending on your audience

1 teaspoon salt
1 teaspoon baking soda dissolved
  in 1 cup hot water

Combine the oil and molasses in a bowl (measure the oil first, then the molasses will come out of the cup more easily). Stir together, then beat in the flour, ginger, and salt. Little by little, mix in the baking soda and water and beat until smooth. Pour into a greased 9-inch-square pan and bake in a preheated oven at 350°F for about 40 minutes, until the ginger bread tests done.

MORE GINGERBREAD

·

½ cup molasses
⅓ cup sugar
½ cup butter, cut into pieces and
  at room temperature
1 cup boiling water
1 egg
1¾ cups flour

1 to 2 tablespoons ground ginger
  (use the larger amount only for
  those with hardy palates)
½ teaspoon ground cinnamon
½ teaspoon ground cloves
1 teaspoon baking soda

$\mathcal{P}$ut the molasses, sugar, and butter in a ceramic mixing bowl. Pour the boiling water over all and stir until the butter is melted. Add the egg and beat well. Combine the flour, ginger, cinnamon, cloves, and baking soda in a small bowl and whisk to blend. Add the flour mixture to the butter mixture and beat until smooth. Pour into a greased 8- or 9-inch-square pan and bake for about 35 minutes, until the gingerbread tests done. If possible, serve warm with whipped cream dusted with nutmeg.

CHEESECAKE

—

We got this recipe from Gordon's aunt, Sally Spiegel, a painter and art teacher. Sally and her husband, Herman, live on the Connecticut shore of Long Island Sound in a house whose spacious kitchen has seen many a potluck supper.

CRUST
1/4 cup butter or margarine
1 cup fine crumbs (zweiback, cookie, or graham cracker)

FILLING
1 1/2 pounds (24 ounces) cream cheese, at room temperature
1 cup sugar
1 teaspoon vanilla
3/4 cup sour cream
4 eggs

TOPPING
1 pint sour cream
1 pint fresh or frozen berries of your choice (Sally usually uses strawberries or blueberries), thawed if frozen
2 tablespoons sugar
1/2 teaspoon vanilla
1 teaspoon cornstarch

For the crust, melt the butter or margarine and stir in the crumbs with a fork. Press firmly onto the bottom and sides of an 8-inch springform pan. Prepare the filling.

In a large bowl or a food processor, combine the cream cheese, sugar, vanilla, and sour cream. Add the eggs one at a time, blending well after each addition. Pour onto the prepared crust and bake in a preheated oven at 350°F for 50 to 55 minutes, until firm in the center. Turn off the heat and let the cake cool in the oven with the door open.

When the cake is cool, prepare the topping.

Mix the sour cream, sugar, and vanilla together and pour over the cooled cake. Return to a preheated 425°F oven and bake for 5 minutes, no longer. The topping will firm up when the cake cools.

To make the berry topping using frozen berries, drain the juice into a small saucepan and add the cornstarch. Bring the mixture to a boil, stirring constantly. Place the drained berries on top of the cake and pour the thickened sauce on top. To use fresh berries, crush 1 cup of the berries in a saucepan. Add the cornstarch and bring to a boil, stirring constantly. Arrange the rest of the fresh berries on top of the cake and pour the thickened sauce on top.

Refrigerate the cake after adding the berry topping. Let come to room temperature before serving.

PUMPKIN-ORANGE
CHEESE PIE

■

This is a light cheesecake, baked in a pastry crust and enlivened with pumpkin pie spices and orange rind.

CRUST

1½ cups flour

¼ teaspoon salt

½ cup lard or other shortening

About 4 tablespoons ice water

FILLING

12 ounces cream cheese, at room temperature

¾ cup brown sugar

2 eggs

1 teaspoon grated orange rind

¼ teaspoon ground nutmeg

1 teaspoon ground cinnamon

One 16-ounce can pumpkin (about 2 cups)

For the crust, combine the flour and salt in a bowl. Cut in the lard, using a pastry blender, until the particles are the size of peas. Add the ice water a tablespoon at a time, mixing with a fork, until the dough just holds together. Form the dough into a ball, flatten into a disk, wrap in plastic, and chill for at least 1 hour. Roll out onto a lightly floured board.

Line a pie pan with the pastry and make a nice fluted edge. In a large bowl with an electric mixer or a food processor, blend the cream cheese and sugar. Beat in the eggs one at a time. Add the orange rind, nutmeg, cinnamon, and pumpkin and beat until smooth. Pour into the pie shell and place in a preheated 425°F oven. Lower the heat to 350°F and bake for about 35 minutes, until the center is almost set. Cool on a wire rack.

MAPLE-PECAN PIE

·

Steve Zakon, author of this recipe, describes it as "less sickeningly sweet than most pecan pies you'll meet. Always a hit at Thanksgiving or Christmas."

3 eggs
¼ cup sugar
¼ teaspoon salt
⅓ cup butter, melted

1½ cups maple syrup
1 cup pecan halves
One 9- or 10-inch pie shell,
  unbaked

In a medium bowl, beat the eggs, then beat in the sugar, salt, butter, and syrup. Stir in the pecans and pour the mixture into the pie shell (page 211). Bake in a preheated oven at 375°F for 45 minutes, until the crust is browned and the pie is firm. Let cool before serving. Top with whipped cream or ice cream at serving time, if desired.

FRESH DEEP-DISH
PEACH PIE

■

We're on the northern edge of peach-tree survival. Once in a while we get a basket of nearly local tree-ripened peaches, enough for a pie or two and a batch of ice cream.

6 cups peeled and sliced ripe *peaches (rock-hard ones will never do)*
1 tablespoon fresh lemon juice
½ cup brown sugar (or to taste)
2 tablespoons cornstarch
1 teaspoon ground ginger

½ teaspoon almond extract
1 tablespoon butter
Pastry for a single top crust for your pie pan (page 211)
Egg wash (1 egg yolk beaten with 1 teaspoon water)
1 tablespoon sugar

𝒫lace the peaches in a medium bowl. Toss with the lemon juice. Sprinkle the brown sugar, cornstarch, ginger, and almond extract over the top. Toss gently to combine. Pile into a 9-inch pie pan or other baking dish. Dot with the butter. Cover with the pastry crust and seal well. Refrigerate while the oven preheats to 425°F. Brush the top of the pie with the egg wash and sprinkle with the sugar. Cut steam vents into the top of the pie. Bake at 425°F for 25 minutes, then reduce the heat to 350°F and bake for another 20 to 25 minutes, until the crust is golden and the smell of the peaches has perfumed your house. Cool the pie on a wire rack. Serve warm or at room temperature.

BLANCHE'S LEMON
MERINGUE PIE

—————
■

Blanche Burnett of Dublin, New Hampshire, gave us this recipe many years ago. Her lemon pie is as famous among pie lovers as her hand-sewn Raggedy Anns and Andys are among children.

1¼ cups sugar
Dash of salt
6 tablespoons cornstarch
1¾ cups boiling water
Grated rind of 1 large lemon
4 tablespoons butter, cut into
  chunks

3 egg yolks
½ cup fresh lemon juice
One 9-inch pie shell, baked to
  golden brown and cooled
  (page 211)

MERINGUE
3 egg whites
Dash of salt

1 teaspoon fresh lemon juice
6 tablespoons sugar

In a heavy saucepan, mix the sugar, salt, and cornstarch. Add the water and lemon rind and cook gently, stirring until thickened. Simmer for 5 minutes. Add the butter, but do not stir. Remove from the heat. Mix the egg yolks and lemon juice. Stir ¼ cup of the hot sugar mixture into the yolks, then pour this mixture back into the saucepan with the sugar mixture. When well blended, pour into the baked pie shell. Bake in a preheated oven at 400°F for 10 minutes while you make the meringue.

Beat the egg whites and salt until soft peaks form. Add the lemon juice. Beat in the sugar gradually until the meringue is stiff but not dry. Spread the meringue over the top of the hot pie to enclose it completely. Continue baking the pie at 350°F until the meringue is lightly browned, 10 to 15 minutes. Serve at room temperature.

CRANBERRY-RAISIN PIE

.

Gordon's grandmother, Doris Morse of Wareham, Massachusetts, lived all of her eighty-four years within a half-mile of her birthplace, also the heart of the cranberry industry. Her husband, Raymond, was a cranberry grower, and Gordon remembers every Thanksgiving dinner featuring cranberries as an indispensable part of the meal. Her Cranberry-Raisin Pie was almost too beautiful to cut into, though no one ever regretted doing so.

1⅓ cups raisins
1⅓ cups cranberries
1 cup sugar
¼ teaspoon salt

1⅓ cups water
1½ tablespoons cornstarch
1 unbaked pie shell and top crust
(page 211)

In a saucepan combine the raisins, cranberries, sugar, salt, and 1 cup of the water. Bring to a boil. Dissolve the cornstarch in the remaining ⅓ cup water and stir into the boiling mixture. Stir constantly until the mixture is thickened (about 2 minutes). Remove from the heat. Allow the mixture to cool slightly, then pour into the unbaked pie shell. Add the top crust: A lattice-work top looks particularly nice over the red filling. Bake in a preheated oven at 350°F for 1 hour.

OUR FAVORITE APPLE PIE

■

This pie can be quite juicy—for apple pie, we join those who say that flour belongs in the crust, not the pie. We started making lard-based crusts only recently; it simply makes the best crust. For those who are watching their cholesterol (i.e., watching it go up), substitute two-thirds cup plus two tablespoons vegetable shortening for the lard. (Lard has more shortening power, so you need less of it.)

CRUST
2 cups flour
½ teaspoon salt

⅔ cup lard
About 6 tablespoons ice water

FILLING
*4 cups peeled and sliced tart
 apples*
1 tablespoon lemon juice
1 teaspoon grated lemon rind
*1 cup sugar (more or less
 according to tartness of apples)*

*1 teaspoon ground cinnamon (or
 to taste)*
1 tablespoon cold butter
2 tablespoons cream

For the crust, combine the flour and salt in a bowl. Cut in the lard, using a pastry blender, until the particles are the size of peas. Add the ice water a tablespoon at a time, mixing with a fork, until the dough just holds together. Form the dough into 2 balls, one slightly larger. Flatten into disks, wrap in plastic, and chill for at least 1 hour. Use the larger disk for the bottom crust.

For the filling, toss the apples with the lemon juice and rind. Add the sugar and cinnamon and toss gently to blend. Roll out the pastry for the bottom crust and place in a pie pan. Heap the apple filling into the crust, keeping the filling higher in the center. Dot with the butter. Roll out the top crust and place on top of the filling, pressing gently. Seal the edges and flute them. Decorate the top of the pie with pastry scraps, if desired, and cut steam vents. Spread the cream over the top of the pie with your fingers or a pastry brush. Place the pie on a pizza pan or other baking sheet to catch bubbling juices. Bake in a preheated oven at 400°F for 10 minutes, then reduce the heat to 350°F and bake for another 40 minutes or until the pastry is golden. Cool on a wire rack. Serve warm or at room temperature.

CHOCOLATE-COFFEE
TOFFEE PIE

■

Barbara Fraser, one of our neighbors in Nelson, crafts a mean pie.

CRUST

½ cup shortening

1 cup flour

Dash of salt

¼ cup brown sugar

¾ cup finely chopped walnuts

1 ounce unsweetened chocolate, grated

2 tablespoons water

1 teaspoon vanilla

FILLING

¼ cup butter, at room temperature

¾ cup sugar

1 ounce unsweetened chocolate, melted

2 teaspoons instant coffee powder

2 eggs

TOPPING

2 cups whipping cream

2 teaspoons instant coffee powder

½ cup confectioners sugar

*F*or the crust, cut the shortening into the flour and salt in a medium bowl. With a fork, add the brown sugar, walnuts, and grated chocolate. Toss with the water and vanilla to make a crumbly dough. Press the dough firmly into a 9-inch pie pan and bake in a preheated oven at 375°F for 15 minutes. Let cool while you make the filling.

Beat the butter until creamy. Gradually add the sugar and beat until light and fluffy. Blend in the melted chocolate and coffee powder. Add the eggs one at a time, beating until well mixed. Pour into the cooled pie shell and refrigerate for several hours or overnight.

Combine all the topping ingredients in a bowl and refrigerate for 1 hour. Beat until stiff and pile onto the pie. Serve immediately, or refrigerate until ready to serve.

CHESS PIE

·

Gordon's sister, Celeste Hewson, got this recipe from her friend Grace Jones of Burwood, Tennessee. Celeste told us that the *Burwood Community Cookbook* has thirteen recipes for Chess Pie—it's a must at covered-dish dinners.

1 cup butter, melted
3 cups sugar
8 eggs

3 tablespoons vinegar
3 tablespoons cornmeal
2 unbaked pie shells (page 216)

Mix the butter, sugar, eggs, vinegar, and cornmeal. Beat until smooth. Divide the batter between the 2 pie shells. Bake in a preheated oven at 350°F until firm, about 45 minutes.

BOILED CIDER PIE

·

We got this recipe from Carolyn Edwards, an editor and a caterer —what a winning combination!

¾ cup brown sugar
4 tablespoons flour
1 egg
2 tablespoons vinegar
6 to 7 tablespoons boiled cider
 (made by boiling 2 cups apple
 cider down to about ½ cup)

Butter the size of a walnut (about
 3 tablespoons)
½ teaspoon ground nutmeg
Pastry for a double-crust pie
 (page 216)

Beat the brown sugar, flour, egg, and vinegar together in a medium bowl. Add the warm boiled cider, butter, and nutmeg. Roll out the bottom crust and press into a pie pan. Pour in the cider filling. Roll out the top crust and place on top of the pie filling. Seal the edges and cut steam vents. Bake in a preheated oven at 350°F for 35 to 40 minutes, until golden brown.

RASPBERRY PIE

·

For a few years, Susan's grandmother-who-lived-next-door, Helen Michaels, had a huge raspberry patch, and Susan remembers helping pick berries on hot summer mornings and selling them for twenty-five cents a quart. There was always enough left over for a pie.

1 unbaked pie shell (page 211)	1 tablespoon flour
1 quart raspberries	2 eggs
1 cup sugar	2 tablespoons milk or light cream

Fill the pie shell with the raspberries. Mix the sugar and flour together and pour evenly over the berries. Beat the eggs and the milk or cream and pour over the berries. Bake in a preheated oven at 350°F for about 45 minutes, until the crust is golden and the custard starts to set.

JOHN'S DELIGHT (STEAMED PUDDING)

—

Our friend Kathy Miller, singer, teacher, and mother of Linnet, Willie, and Owen, inherited this traditional recipe from her grandmother, Margaret Hitchcock Green, who served it to the family every Christmas dinner. Steamed puddings may be made ahead of time and resteamed for a half hour or so before going to a potluck.

2 cups chopped bread or cake
½ cup butter, melted
½ cup molasses
½ cup raisins
1 cup milk

1 egg
½ teaspoon baking soda
½ teaspoon ground cloves
½ teaspoon ground cinnamon

Combine all the ingredients and pour the batter into a buttered pudding mold. (A coffee can will do, as long as it holds the batter with at least 1 inch to spare. Cover with waxed paper or aluminum foil held in place by a rubber band.) Cover and steam on a trivet over 1 inch gently boiling water for 1½ to 2 hours. Uncover the pudding and let it rest before unmolding. Serve warm. The pudding is extra special with ice cream, hard sauce, or whipped cream.

BAKED APPLE PUDDING
WITH RUM SAUCE

■

Mary Sheldon got this recipe from Dorothy Hargrove of Mississippi in 1954 and has the recipe card to prove it.

PUDDING

1 cup flour
1 teaspoon baking soda
1 teaspoon baking powder
1 teaspoon ground cinnamon
¾ teaspoon ground nutmeg
¼ teaspoon salt

¼ cup butter, at room
  temperature
1 cup sugar
1 egg, beaten
2 cups grated unpeeled apples

RUM SAUCE

½ cup butter
1 cup sugar
½ cup light cream
Dash of ground nutmeg

1 teaspoon vanilla
2 to 3 tablespoons rum or 1
  teaspoon rum flavoring (or to
  taste)

For the pudding, sift together the flour, baking soda, baking powder, cinnamon, nutmeg, and salt. In a medium bowl, cream the butter and sugar. Add the beaten egg and grated apples. Add the flour mixture and stir to combine. Pour into a greased 9-inch-square pan and bake in a preheated oven at 400°F for about 25 minutes. Serve warm or at room temperature with the warm rum sauce.

For the sauce, mix the butter, sugar, and cream in the top of a double boiler and cook over simmering water until thickened. Remove from the heat and stir in the nutmeg, vanilla, and rum or rum flavoring.

DUTCH APPLE KUCHEN

— ▪

This is another old favorite from Susan's grandmother, Helen Michaels. We think it came from Grandma's mother, Katherine Kaltenbrun of Saint Nazianz, Wisconsin.

1¼ cups flour
1 teaspoon baking powder
½ teaspoon salt
2 tablespoons sugar
½ cup butter, at room
  temperature

1 egg yolk beaten with
  2 tablespoons milk
6 cups peeled and sliced apples

TOPPING
¾ cup sugar
1 tablespoon flour

½ teaspoon ground cinnamon
3 tablespoons butter

Sift together the flour, baking powder, and salt. Cream the sugar and butter. Add the flour mixture alternately with the egg yolk and milk mixture, stirring with a fork. The mixture will be crumbly. Pat into a 9-by-13-inch pan. Fill with the apple slices.

For the topping, combine the sugar, flour, and cinnamon in a small bowl. Cut in the butter until the mixture is in coarse crumbs. Sprinkle on top of the apples and bake in a preheated oven at 350°F for about 30 minutes, until the apples are tender.

SCHAUM TORTE

— ▪

We got this recipe from Margaret Mahnke, Susan's mother. (Thanks, Mom.) To transport this any distance, bring the baked meringue, fruit, and whipping cream separately. Assemble the torte and whip the cream when you reach your destination.

6 egg whites, at room temperature
⅛ teaspoon (a pinch) cream of
  tartar
2 cups sugar
1 tablespoon white vinegar

1 teaspoon vanilla
1 quart fresh berries (Mom
  usually uses sliced strawberries)
1 cup whipping cream

*B*eat the egg whites until frothy. Add the cream of tartar. Beat until very stiff, adding the sugar gradually until all the sugar is incorporated. Mix in the vinegar and vanilla. Spoon into an ungreased springform pan and bake in a preheated oven at 325°F for 1 hour. Let cool.

To assemble, remove the meringue from the pan and split in half horizontally. Place the bottom half on a serving plate. Fill with the fruit and add the top layer of meringue. Whip the cream and spoon on top. Garnish with additional fruit if desired. Cut into wedges.

CHERRY TORTE

•

Folksinger Sally Rogers sent this to us; she got it from her aunt Dorothy Kraker. "This recipe," Sally writes, "is especially reminiscent of my childhood on the cherry orchard and of course should be made with Michigan cherries. It's *really easy*."

1 tablespoon butter, at room
  temperature
1 cup sugar
1 egg
1 cup flour

1 teaspoon baking powder
½ teaspoon salt
1 cup drained sour cherries
  (frozen or canned, preferably
  juice-packed)

*C*ream the butter and sugar. Stir in the egg. Add the flour, baking powder, and salt to make a dry batter. Fold in the cherries and place in a greased 8-inch-square cake pan. Bake in a preheated oven at 325°F for about 45 minutes. Test with a toothpick for doneness. Serve warm with whipped cream or vanilla ice cream.

CRANAPPLE CRUNCH

.

1 cup sugar
¾ cup water
1½ to 2 cups cranberries
4 to 5 apples, peeled and thinly
  sliced

4 tablespoons lemon juice
1½ cups rolled oats
¾ cup brown sugar
½ cup butter, melted
1½ tablespoons flour

ℬring the sugar and water to a boil in a medium saucepan. Add the cranberries and cook until the skins pop. Toss the apples in the lemon juice and place in a 9-inch pie pan. Pour the cranberry mixture over the apples. Mix the oats, brown sugar, butter, and flour in a small bowl until crumbly. Sprinkle over the fruit. Bake in a preheated oven at 350°F for 35 to 40 minutes. Serve warm.

GINGERED APPLE CRISP

.

4 to 5 large apples, peeled and
  sliced (or enough to fill a pie
  plate)
1 tablespoon lemon juice
¼ cup sugar
½ cup butter, melted

½ cup brown sugar
¾ cup rolled oats
½ cup flour
1 teaspoon ground ginger
1 to 2 tablespoons chopped
  crystallized ginger

𝒯oss the apples with the lemon juice and sugar and put in a pie plate. In a medium bowl, combine the melted butter, brown sugar, rolled oats, flour, and ground ginger. Toss until well blended and crumbly. Add the crystallized ginger and toss. Sprinkle the oat mixture over the apples and pat down. Bake in a preheated oven at 350°F for about 45 minutes. Serve warm. Vanilla ice cream or frozen yogurt goes well.

JUDY'S BAKLAVA

■

While Joel Patenaude was spending his high school senior year (1988–89) in Istanbul, Turkey, on a Rotary youth exchange, his family at home in Mount Horeb, Wisconsin, was missing him. Judy, his mother, decided to make baklava for Christmas dinner, bringing Joel home at least in spirit. This version is not as sweet as the baklava served in American Middle-Eastern restaurants, but we know it is authentic: It passed the Joel test when he returned home a self-proclaimed baklava expert.

2 cups chopped walnuts
½ cup sugar
2 teaspoons ground cinnamon
1 cup butter, melted

One 8-ounce package phyllo
   pastry, thawed (see page 151)
½ cup honey, warmed

Combine the walnuts, sugar, and cinnamon in a bowl and set aside. Using a pastry brush or paint brush, butter the bottom of a cookie sheet or 9-by-13-inch pan. Working quickly so the phyllo doesn't dry out, place 3 sheets of phyllo in the pan, then paint liberally with the butter. Repeat until half of the phyllo is used. Spread the filling evenly over the buttered phyllo. Then repeat layering the phyllo and buttering, ending with an unbuttered sheet of phyllo. Cut the baklava into triangles or diamonds, then butter the top layer thoroughly. Bake in a preheated oven at 350°F for 20 to 25 minutes, until golden. Remove from the oven and gently brush the warmed honey over the top. Cool and eat. Your friends will assume you worked your fingers to the bone to prepare something so exotic.

GREAT-AUNT RUBY'S
CHOCOLATE TEA CAKES

■

We got this treasure from our friend Julie Brody, who told us its history: "My great-aunt Ruby Hoffman, who gave me this recipe, was the head of the Lever Brothers' Spry test kitchens in Cambridge during the 1930s and 1940s. Her real specialty was pie crusts. The only thing *I don't* like about taking G.A.R.'s tea cakes to a potluck is that someone *always* asks me for the recipe, and then I have to show them that the ingredients aren't exactly the healthy foods you want your good friends to be eating. On the other hand, Great-Aunt Ruby lived to be ninety years old and her sister Maude (my granny, who did far more than her share of the eating) is still going strong at one hundred, even though the two of them subsisted on Ruby's finest pies, fudge, tea cakes, and the like."

1 cup butter or margarine, at
  room temperature
1/3 cup sugar
5 tablespoons unsweetened cocoa
1 egg, slightly beaten
1 teaspoon vanilla
2 cups graham cracker crumbs

1 cup coconut
3/4 cup chopped nuts
3/4 cup confectioners sugar
2 teaspoons milk or cream
2 squares unsweetened baking
  chocolate

Melt half of the butter or margarine. Add the sugar, cocoa, egg, and vanilla. Fold in the graham cracker crumbs, coconut, and chopped nuts. Press into an 8-by-8-inch pan. Set aside 1 teaspoon of the remaining shortening and cream the rest with the confectioners sugar and the milk or cream. Spread this mixture over the first layer and refrigerate for at least 2 hours. Melt the unsweetened chocolate with the reserved teaspoon of butter. Add the vanilla. Pour over the other layers and refrigerate until the chocolate is solid. Using a sharp knife, cut the tea cakes into 12 to 16 pieces.

For easy transportation, cut the tea cakes at home, but leave them in the pan. In very hot weather, put the pan of tea cakes in the freezer for an hour or so before you leave home.

This recipe won the "Most Outrageous" award at the Newton Highlands (Massachusetts) Village Day bake sale last spring.

—J. B.

LEMON   BARS

•

Sharon Smith brought these bars to several cookie exchanges at Christmas time.

CRUST
1 cup butter, at room temperature   ½ cup sugar
2⅔ cups flour

LEMON FILLING
4 eggs   Grated rind of 1 lemon
1½ cups sugar   Confectioners sugar for dusting
½ teaspoon baking powder   bars
6 tablespoons lemon juice

For the crust, combine the butter, flour, and sugar using a pastry blender and mix until well blended. Pat into a greased 9-by-13-inch pan and bake in a preheated oven at 350°F to 15 to 20 minutes. Meanwhile, make the lemon filling.

Beat the eggs. Stir in the sugar, baking powder, lemon juice, and lemon rind. Mix thoroughly and pour over the hot crust. Return to the oven and bake 18 to 20 minutes more. Remove from the oven and cool on a wire rack. Dust with confectioners sugar when cool. Cut into bars. Makes about 50 1-by-2-inch bars.

LINDY'S GINGER COOKIES

·

This recipe makes soft cookies. The dough can be rolled out and cut with cookie cutters or dropped from a spoon. We got the recipe from Lindy Black.

½ cup butter or margarine, at
  room temperature
1 cup sugar
2 eggs
1 cup molasses
½ cup soured milk or buttermilk
  (1½ teaspoons lemon juice plus
  milk to make ½ cup)

2 teaspoons ground ginger
2 teaspoons baking soda
3¾ to 4 cups flour

Cream the shortening and sugar; add the eggs and molasses and mix well. Stir in the soured milk or buttermilk. Sift the ginger, baking soda, and flour together. Add to the butter mixture and work into a soft dough. Roll out on a lightly floured board (don't add too much extra flour) and cut out with a cookie cutter or drop from a spoon. Bake in a preheated oven at 350°F for about 10 minutes. Makes about 4 dozen cookies.

MORE GINGER COOKIES

·

These (usually) come out thin and crisp, with a crinkled top.

¾ cup butter or margarine, at
  room temperature
2 cups sugar
2 eggs, beaten
½ cup molasses
2 teaspoons vinegar

3¾ cups flour
1½ teaspoons baking soda
1 tablespoon ground ginger
½ teaspoon ground cinnamon
½ teaspoon ground cloves
½ teaspoon ground nutmeg

Cream the shortening and sugar. Add the eggs, molasses, and vinegar and blend well. Sift the flour, baking soda, ginger, cinnamon, cloves, and nutmeg together and add to the butter mixture. Mix thoroughly. Shape the dough into balls about 1 inch in diameter and place on cookie sheets. Bake in a preheated oven at 350°F for about 10 minutes, until the cookies are golden. Remove from the oven and leave on the cookie sheets for about 1 minute, then remove to wire racks to cool. Makes about 4 dozen cookies.

MAPLE-PECAN
LACE COOKIES

·

This is a New England variation on your basic lace cookie. The cookies are somewhat fragile but make an elegant addition to a dessert table.

½ cup maple syrup
⅓ cup butter

½ cup flour
½ cup finely chopped pecans

Place the maple syrup and butter in a saucepan over low heat. Boil for 30 seconds. Let cool to room temperature. Stir in the flour and pecans. Drop by teaspoonfuls onto greased cookie sheets, leaving at least 3 inches between each cookie. Bake in a preheated oven at 325°F for 8 to 10 minutes. Cool in the pans for 1 minute, then remove immediately with a spatula and place on wire racks or brown paper. Makes about 2 dozen cookies.

BARBARA FRASER'S
FROSTED APPLE COOKIES

■

1 cup butter, at room temperature
2⅔ cups brown sugar
2 eggs
1 teaspoon ground cloves
1 teaspoon ground nutmeg
2 teaspoons ground cinnamon
4 cups flour
2 teaspoons baking soda

½ teaspoon salt
2 cups peeled and chopped apples
1 cup chopped walnuts
1 cup raisins
½ cup milk
1½ cups confectioners sugar
  mixed with enough milk to make
  a thin icing

Cream the butter and brown sugar. Add the eggs and spices. In a separate bowl, whisk together the flour, baking soda, and salt. Add half of the flour mixture to the butter mixture, then add the apples, walnuts, and raisins. Add the milk and the rest of the flour mixture. Drop by spoonfuls onto cookies sheets and bake in a pre-heated oven at 375°F for about 10 minutes. Remove to wire racks. Glaze with the confectioners sugar icing while still warm. Makes about 4 dozen cookies.

BEACON HILL BROWNIES

■

If you really want to gild the lily, apply frosting.

8 ounces unsweetened chocolate
1 cup butter, at room temperature
5 eggs
3 cups sugar

1 tablespoon vanilla
1½ cups flour
2 cups broken walnuts (optional)

elt the chocolate and butter in a heavy saucepan over low heat, stirring to combine. Cool. Beat the eggs, sugar, and vanilla for 10 minutes in a large bowl using an electric mixer. Blend in the chocolate mixture. Add the flour and stir in by hand just until blended. Fold in the nuts if desired. Spread in a greased 9-by-13-inch pan and bake in a preheated oven at 375°F for 35 to 40 minutes, until the top is dull and cracked around the edges. Do not overbake or the brownies will dry out. Cool in the pan on a wire rack. Cut when completely cool. Makes about 2 dozen 2-inch-square brownies.

BLONDIES

·

This recipe can be doubled for large suppers and school bake sales. Alice and Castle Freeman brought this dessert to the potluck supper at our wedding.

2 cups flour	2 cups brown sugar
1½ teaspoons baking powder	2 eggs
¼ teaspoon salt	2 teaspoons vanilla
½ cup plus 2 tablespoons unsalted butter, at room temperature	1 cup semisweet chocolate chips
	¾ cup chopped walnuts

In a bowl, sift together the flour, baking powder, and salt. In a large bowl with an electric mixer, cream the butter and brown sugar until light and fluffy. Add the eggs one at a time, beating well, and stir in the vanilla. Add the flour mixture and stir until the batter is well blended. Stir in the chocolate chips and walnuts. Scrape the batter into a buttered and floured 9-by-13-inch pan, smooth the top, and bake in a preheated oven at 350°F for 30 to 35 minutes, until the bars pull away slightly from the sides of the pan and the center is firm. Cool in the pan on a wire rack before cutting into serving pieces. Makes about 24 two-inch-square servings.

CRÈME DE MENTHE
BROWNIES

·

Both Betsey Church and Julie Rohr gave us recipes for these rich treats. (Nelson is a small town, after all.) We know from experience that they are the first to go at bake sales and church suppers. The bars can be cut fairly small and served in a small cupcake papers. If you use white crème de menthe, add a few drops of green food coloring to the mint layer.

BROWNIE LAYER
4 squares unsweetened baking chocolate
⅔ cup butter
2 cups sugar
4 eggs
1 teaspoon vanilla

1¼ cups flour
1 teaspoon baking powder
½ teaspoon salt
1 cup crushed pecans

CRÈME DE MENTHE LAYER
½ cup butter, at room temperature
2 cups confectioners sugar

2 tablespoons green crème de menthe or 2 teaspoons peppermint extract plus a few drops of green food coloring

CHOCOLATE TOPPING
6 tablespoons butter

1 cup semisweet chocolate chips

For the brownie layer, melt the chocolate and butter in a heavy saucepan. Cool. Add the sugar, eggs, and vanilla and beat well. Add the flour, baking powder, and salt and stir with a wooden spoon just until blended. Add pecans and stir. Pour into a greased 9-by-13-inch pan and bake in a preheated oven at 350°F for 30 minutes. Cool in the pan on a wire rack. (The brownies can be made a day ahead.)

For the crème de menthe layer, place the butter, confectioners sugar, and crème de menthe or peppermint extract in a bowl and beat with an electric mixer until smooth. Spread over the cooled brownies. Refrigerate for one hour.

For the topping, melt the butter and chocolate chips together in the top of a double boiler over simmering water. Stir until smooth, then remove from the heat and let cool. Quickly spread the topping over the crème de menthe layer and return the pan to the refrigerator. Chill the brownies for 1 hour to set up, then cut into small squares. Makes about 4 dozen ½-inch-square brownies.

NUT TARTS

———
■

Susan's mother, Margaret Mahnke, makes these at Christmas time. You could get creative and fill them with something else— anything that goes inside a pie shell is fair game.

TART SHELLS
½ cup butter, at room
  temperature
1 cup flour

3 ounces cream cheese, at room
  temperature

NUT FILLING
¾ cup brown sugar
1 egg
1 tablespoon butter, at room
  temperature

1 cup chopped nuts
½ teaspoon vanilla

For the shells, combine the butter, flour, and cream cheese into a smooth dough and divide into 24 little balls. Press into miniature muffin tins to line the bottoms and sides.

Combine all the filling ingredients in a small bowl and put 1 teaspoon of the mixture in each shell. Bake in a preheated oven at 375°F for about 20 minutes. Makes 24 tarts.

PEANUT SQUARES

■

These are perfect cubes of cake covered with a frosting and rolled in peanuts.

1 cup sugar
½ cup margarine, at room
   temperature, or vegetable
   shortening

¾ cup milk
2 cups flour
2 teaspoons baking powder
3 egg whites, beaten until stiff

FROSTING
¾ cup butter, at room
   temperature
2 cups sifted confectioners sugar

3 egg yolks
1 tablespoon milk (if needed)

2 pounds unsalted peanuts,
   ground or finely chopped

Cream the sugar and shortening. Add the milk alternately with the flour and baking powder and stir until smooth. Fold in the beaten egg whites. Bake in a greased 9-by-13-inch pan in a preheated oven at 350°F for about 25 minutes, until the cake pulls away from the pan at the edges. Cool.

For the frosting, combine the butter, confectioners sugar, and egg yolks and beat until smooth. Add a little milk if the frosting is too stiff. Cut the cake into 2-inch squares. Frost each side of the square (cube, really) and roll in the peanuts until all the surfaces are covered. Place on a cookie sheet or tray to set before serving. Makes about 2 dozen squares.

HERMITS

.

One of my goals in life is to make Hermits like the ones Gordon remembers his Grandmother Morse making him when he was a boy. (We have her recipe, in her very handwriting, but the result "just isn't the same.") The following effort has come closest (so far). It is based on a recipe in Richard Sax's *The Cookie Lover's Cookie Book* (Harper & Row, 1986).

—S.P.

1 cup butter, at room temperature	2 teaspoons ground ginger
2½ cups light-brown sugar	1 teaspoon ground nutmeg
3 eggs	½ teaspoon ground cloves
⅓ cup molasses	½ teaspoon salt
4 cups flour	3 tablespoons finely chopped
1½ teaspoons baking powder	crystallized ginger
1½ teaspoon baking soda	1 cup raisins
1½ teaspoons ground cinnamon	

*C*ream the butter and sugar in an electric mixer until light. Add the eggs one at a time, beating well after each addition, then add the molasses. Sift the flour, baking powder, baking soda, cinnamon, ginger, nutmeg, cloves, and salt together. Add to the butter mixture and stir just until blended. Stir in the crystallized ginger and the raisins. Using moistened fingers, shape the dough into 6 logs (2 each on 3 cookie sheets) about 1 inch high and 1½ inches wide; length depends on the baker! The dough will spread out as it bakes, so leave enough space. Bake in a preheated oven at 375°F, one sheet at a time, for about 12 minutes, until the hermits are golden brown but still soft. (If you overbake them, they won't be chewy.) Use a large spatula to remove the logs to wire racks to cool, then slice on the diagonal into bars about 2 inches wide. Store in a tightly covered container.

LEMON SUGAR COOKIES

■

These cookies are crisp and have a nice crackly top.

2¾ cups flour
2 tablespoons baking powder
¼ teaspoon salt
1 cup butter, at room temperature
2 cups sugar

2 eggs
1 tablespoon grated lemon rind
3 tablespoons fresh lemon juice
1 cup quick rolled oats

Sift the flour, baking powder, and salt together. In a large bowl, cream the butter and sugar. Add the eggs and beat well. Add the lemon rind and juice to the butter mixture. Gradually add the flour mixture, then the oats. Blend well, then chill the dough for at least 2 hours. Roll teaspoonfuls of the dough into balls and place on greased cookie sheets, allowing room for the cookies to spread. Using a flat-bottomed glass or a custard cup that has been greased and dipped in sugar, flatten each ball to ¼-inch thickness. (Dip the glass in sugar each time.) Bake in a preheated oven at 375°F until lightly browned around the edges, about 8 to 10 minutes. Cool on the cookie sheets for 1 minute, then carefully remove and cool on racks. Makes about 40 cookies.

CHOCOLATE OATMEAL
BARS

___
■

These are rich, so you can cut them small (and eat two or three!).

CHOCOLATE FILLING
2 tablespoons butter
1 cup semisweet chocolate chips
One 5⅓-ounce can evaporated
  milk or light cream

¼ cup sugar
½ cup chopped nuts

COOKIE BASE
½ cup butter, at room
  temperature
1 cup brown sugar
1 egg

1 teaspoon vanilla
1¼ cups flour
½ teaspoon baking soda
2 cups quick rolled oats

For the filling, combine the butter, chocolate chips, evaporated milk or cream, and sugar in a heavy saucepan. Bring to a rolling boil, stirring constantly. Remove from the heat. Stir in the nuts and cool.

For the cookie base, cream the butter and sugar. Add the egg and vanilla and beat until light. Stir in the flour, baking soda, and 1¾ cups of the oats until well blended. Press two thirds of this mixture into the bottom of a buttered 9-inch-square pan. Spread with the cooled chocolate filling. Mix the remaining ¼ cup oats with the remainder of the cookie base and crumble over the filling. Bake in a preheated oven at 350°F for 25 to 30 minutes. Cool in the pan on a wire rack before cutting into bars of desired size.

BUTTERCRUNCH BARS

■

A nice mixture of butterscotch and chocolate flavors.

1 cup butter, melted
1 cup brown sugar
1 egg, separated
1 teaspoon vanilla
2 cups flour

Pinch of salt
1 cup finely chopped walnuts or
  pecans
1 cup semisweet chocolate chips

Combine the melted butter and brown sugar and stir well. Add the egg yolk and vanilla and blend. Stir in the flour and salt. The dough will be moist. Pat the dough into a 15-by-10-by-1-inch jelly-roll pan. Stir the egg white with a fork and brush onto the dough. Sprinkle evenly with the chopped nuts and chocolate chips. Bake in a preheated oven at 375°F for about 20 minutes, until the crust is golden brown. Cool in the pan on a wire rack and cut into bars of desired size.

DARK SPICED SHORTBREAD

■

1 cup butter, at room temperature
1 cup dark-brown sugar
1½ tablespoons grated orange
  rind
2 tablespoons ground ginger

2 teaspoons ground cinnamon
¾ teaspoon ground cloves
1 teaspoon baking soda
Dash of salt
2 cups flour

Cream the butter and sugar in a large bowl with an electric mixer until light. Add the orange rind, ginger, cinnamon, cloves, baking soda, and salt and beat well. Add the flour and mix just until blended. Divide the dough between two 8- or 9-inch round cake pans (ungreased) and press down firmly. Bake in a preheated oven at 325°F for about 25 minutes, until the tops look dry and the edges are slightly higher than the centers. Cool in the pans for about 5 minutes, then cut into small wedges and continue cooling in the pans.

BEN WATSON'S
CHOCOLATE TRUFFLES

———

•

Ben, who used to live in Nelson, and now lives and works in Williamstown, Massachusetts, gave these out at Christmastime a few years back.

1 cup semisweet chocolate chips
¼ cup confectioners sugar
3 tablespoons butter
3 egg yolks, slightly beaten
1 tablespoon brandy or rum or
* 2 teaspoons vanilla*

¼ cup finely chopped walnuts
* (optional)*
2 ounces semisweet chocolate,
* grated*
½ teaspoon ground cinnamon

In a double boiler over hot water, melt the chocolate chips with the confectioners sugar and butter. Remove from the heat. Slowly stir a small amount of the melted mixture into the egg yolks, then return this mixture to the chocolate mixture and stir well. Blend in the brandy, rum, or vanilla. Add the chopped nuts if desired. Chill this mixture for 1 to 2 hours without stirring. Mix the grated chocolate and cinnamon on a plate. Form the truffle mixture into 1-inch balls and roll the balls in the grated chocolate mixture. Store the truffles in the refrigerator. Serve in small muffin papers or candy cups.

STRAWBERRY SALAD

·

Merle Peery got this recipe from a friend in South Carolina, Betty Lewis, who is a minister's wife and knows all about church suppers!

One 6-ounce package strawberry
 Jell-O
2 cups boiling water
One 10-ounce package frozen
 sliced strawberries with juice

1 large (20-ounce) can crushed
 pineapple with juice
1 cup sour cream

Combine the Jell-O and water and stir until the Jell-O melts. Add the frozen strawberries and stir to melt. Add the pineapple and mix well. Allow to thicken in the refrigerator until nearly firm. Spoon half of the mixture into a greased 6-cup mold or a 9-inch-square cake pan. Top with the sour cream in a smooth layer. Spoon the remaining half of the Jell-O mixture over the sour cream. Chill until firm. Unmold if necessary and cut into squares.

FOOLPROOF FUDGE

·

Mary Bevilacqua and Laurel Gabel gave us this recipe several years ago. It makes a smooth, never grainy, fudge.

3 cups semisweet chocolate chips
One 15-ounce can sweetened
 condensed milk

1½ teaspoons vanilla
½ cup chopped nuts

Melt the chocolate chips in a heavy pan over very low heat. Stir until smooth. Remove from the heat. Stir in the sweetened condensed milk, vanilla, and nuts until well blended. Spread in an 8-inch-square pan lined with buttered waxed paper. Chill for several hours. Invert the pan onto a cutting board, peel off the paper, and cut the fudge into small squares.